People Who Changed
American History

100
Native
Americans
Who Changed
American History

Bonnie Juettner

WORLD ALMANAC® LIBRARY

Please visit our web site at: www.garethstevens.com
For a free color catalog describing our list of high-quality books,
call 1-800-542-2595 (USA) or 1-800-387-3178 (Canada).

Library of Congress Cataloging-in-Publication Data

Juettner, Bonnie.
   100 Native Americans who changed American history / by Bonnie Juettner.
     p. cm. — (People who changed American history)
   Includes index.
   ISBN-13: 978-0-8368-5770-2 (lib. bdg.)
   ISBN-10: 0-8368-5770-4 (lib. bdg.)
   1. Indians of North America—Biography—Juvenile literature. I. Title: One hundred
Native Americans who changed American history. II. Juettner, Bonnie. 100 Native Americans
who shaped American history. III. Title. IV. Series.
  E89.J84 2005
  920'.009297—dc22
  [B]   2004057741

This North American edition first published in 2005 by
World Almanac® Library
An imprint of Gareth Stevens Publishing
1 Reader's Digest Road
Pleasantville, NY 10570-7000 USA

This U.S. edition © 2005 by World Almanac® Library. Original edition © 2003 by Bluewood Books.
First published by Bluewood Books, A Division of The Siyeh Group, Inc., P.O. Box 689, San Mateo, CA 94401.

Editor: Tony Napoli
Indexer: Barbara Cross
Designer: Kevin Harris
World Almanac® Library editor: Jim Mezzanotte
World Almanac® Library art direction and cover design: Tammy West

Cover image: LaDonna Harris

Photo credits: All illustrations and photos courtesy of the Bluewood Archives; Bureau of Indian Affairs; Library of
Congress; National Archives; Smithsonian Institution; U.S. Indian Service; U.S. Park Service and the U.S. Senate, with
the following exceptions: 94: Alyeska Pipeline Service Co.; 80: Americans for Indian Opportunity, LaDonna Harris;
33: Arizona Pioneers Historical Association; 89: Arizona State University; 50: Baylor University; 83: Fred Begay; 41:
Burlingame Public Library; 51: Chief Plenty Coups State Park; 66: Cumberland County Historical Society; 72:
Dr. Theodore Hetzel; 73: © Frank Edwards/Fotos International/Getty Images; 104: Hulleah Tsinhnahjinnie; 81:
Institute of American Indian Art; 76: © Hulton Archive/Getty Images; 17: Dave Jackson; 77: Betty Mae Tiger Jumper;
57: Kansas State Historical Society; 87: © Giulio Marcocchi/Getty Images; 102: Robert Megginson; 90: Billy Mills
Speakers Bureau; 34: Museum of New Mexico; 64: © National Baseball Hall of Fame Library/MLB Photos via Getty
Images; 100: Native American Rights Fund; 52, 58, 60: Nebraska State Historical Society; 49: Nevada State Museum;
16, 19: New York Historical Society; 82: Nowa Cumig Institute; 98: Leonard Peltier Defense Committee; 106: © Keri
Pickett Photography; 105: © Keri Pickett/Time & Life Pictures/Getty Images; 18: Marian Bailey Presswood; 91:
Rainbow Youth & Family Services; 107: © Rex Rystedt/MPI/Getty Images; 93: Tama Rothchild Photography; 103:
Seaver Books; 69: South Dakota State Historical Society-State Archives; 28: State Historical Society of Colorado; 24:
State Historical Society of North Dakota; 101: Sammy Still, Cherokee Nation; 63, 67, 74, 85, 92, 97, 99: Zimou Larry
Tan; 95: University of Arizona Press; 30: University of Oklahoma Library; 29: University of Wyoming, American
Heritage Center.

Printed in the United States of America

About the Author: Bonnie Juettner is a freelance writer and grew up in McGrath, Alaska, an Upper Kuskokwim Athabascan
village in Alaska's interior, and currently lives in Chicago, Illinois. She has written biographies for several reference books,
and writes and edits social studies materials for educational textbooks and videos. This is her second book.

TABLE OF CONTENTS

1500   **1800**

TABLE OF CONTENTS

1801   **1850**

TABLE OF CONTENTS

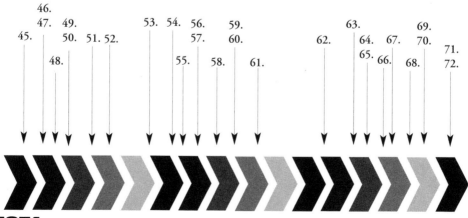

46.
47. 49.
45.   50. 51. 52.   53. 54. 56.   59.   63.   69.
      48.   57.   60.   62.   64. 67.   70.   71.
                        55.   58.   61.   65. 66.   68.   72.

1851   1930

TABLE OF CONTENTS

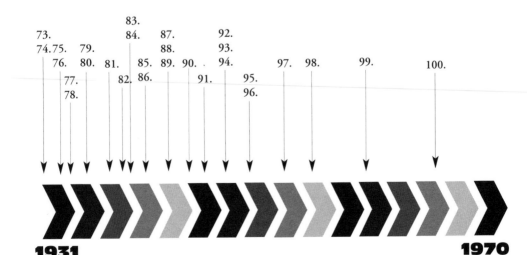

73.
74.75.   79.
    76.   80.   81.
        77.
        78.

83.
84.   87.   92.
    88.   93.
85.   89.   90.   94.
82.   86.   91.   95.
                96.

97.   98.   99.   100.

1931   1970

ALPHABETICAL
TABLE OF CONTENTS

1. Dekanawida
(c. 1550–c. 1600)

Dekanawida was the founder of the legendary Iroquois Confederacy. The exact years during which he lived are not known, but historians do know several things about his life. He was born in present-day Ontario, Canada. According to legend, when Dekanawida was a baby, his mother dreamed that he would someday destroy their nation, the Hurons. So she and his grandmother tried three times to drown him, but the morning after each attempt, they woke to find him sleeping peacefully in his mother's arms. Finally, his mother resigned herself to raising Dekanawida to adulthood.

Hiawatha

As an adult, Dekanawida crossed Lake Ontario to what later became New York State. There, he met Hiawatha, an Onondaga from a Mohawk community, who became his friend and spokesperson. (According to legend, Dekanawida had a speech impediment that made him stutter severely.) Together, they planned to bring peace to the Native American tribes in the area. Then, Hiawatha carried Dekanawida's ideas to the Mohawks, Cayugas, Oneidas, Onondagas, and Senecas, who had been fiercely fighting among themselves for years.

Under Dekanawida's plan, the Iroquois Confederacy became famous for its democratic structures and for the dignity and statesmanship of its leaders. Confederacy leaders were commonly known as chiefs, but some historians believe they were more like chairmen. Chiefs could not promote their own personal points of view. Instead, they had to carefully represent the interests of their communities. If chiefs did not remain faithful to the interests of their communities, they were removed from office.

In his Great Law, Dekanawida gave men and women roughly equal amounts of power in tribal society. While all chiefs were men, they were chosen by women. In special circumstances, however, men could be elected to office by the chiefs themselves. Women owned the land and the soil. Minorities in Iroquois society were protected from discrimination because Iroquois laws were not passed by majority vote. A policy could not become law unless it was agreed upon unanimously. For his role in ending wars between the nations, Dekanawida is often called "The Peacemaker."

Iroquois laws and the Iroquois system of government might seem familiar to Americans. Several founders of the United States—Benjamin Franklin and Thomas Jefferson among them—admired the Iroquois form of government. In 1754, Franklin drew up his Albany Plan, a document designed to unite the thirteen colonies as a federation modeled on Iroquois institutions. Franklin's plan was not ratified, but it later became the model for the Articles of Confederation, the predecessor to the U.S. Constitution.

Dekanawida's Iroquois Confederacy became the most powerful Native American confederation in North America, and it lasted for hundreds of years. Dekanawida achieved his goal—he brought the Iroquois tribes a lasting peace.

2. Squanto
(c. 1580–1622)

Squanto, also known as Tisquantum, was the translator and guide sent by the Wampanoag leader Massasoit (see no. 3) to help the Pilgrims during their first few years in North America.

Historians know little about Squanto's early life. He was a member of the Pawtuxet tribe, one of many Algonquian-speaking tribes of present-day New England. Some historians believe that English explorers kidnapped him and took him to England in 1605, and that he returned with John Smith in 1614. After Smith left, Squanto and twenty other Pawtuxet were kidnapped by explorer Thomas Hunt. Hunt took them to Spain and sold them as slaves, but Squanto was rescued by Spanish friars. He went to England and began working for English explorers, perhaps as an indentured servant. He traveled to Newfoundland in 1617 and came home to the Pawtuxet area, in Massachusetts Bay, in 1619.

An epidemic had swept through the region in his absence, and Squanto found his village abandoned. Most Pawtuxet had died or moved away. When his employer was killed in a battle with the Wampanoag, Squanto became a prisoner of Massasoit. When the Pilgrims settled Plymouth Colony, Massasoit sent Squanto and another English-speaking prisoner of war, Samoset, to talk to them. After Squanto translated when Massasoit and Pilgrim leaders negotiated a treaty, he remained in Plymouth Colony.

Most of the English settlers had not been farmers in England. Squanto taught them how to plant corn and other native vegetables, because their seeds of English barley, wheat, and peas did not thrive in New England. He also taught the colonists to make fish traps and guided them as they explored the region.

Squanto continued to serve as a translator when the Pilgrims needed to communicate with Massasoit and with other Native American tribes in the area. The Pilgrims were relieved to have Squanto's help. William Bradford, one of the Plymouth Colony's governors, described him as "a special instrument sent of God for their good beyond their expectation."

Some historians believe that Squanto was hoping to use his friendship with the Pilgrims to gain political power. He may have hoped to replace Massasoit as the leader of the Wampanoag. In 1621, Squanto told the English that Massasoit was planning to attack the colony. In reality, Massasoit had no plans to attack, and Squanto's lie nearly destroyed the peace between Plymouth Colony and the Wampanoag.

When Squanto's deceit was discovered, Massasoit demanded his execution, but the Pilgrims depended on him so heavily that they protected him. The following year, Squanto became ill and died while he was guiding Bradford on a trip around Cape Cod.

Squanto

Massasoit was the leader of the Wampanoag, one of many Algonquian-speaking tribes that once lived in present-day New England. He helped the Pilgrims survive their first winters in the region. Massasoit negotiated a treaty with the new settlers, and he maintained peace between his tribe and the Plymouth Colony throughout his lifetime.

When the Pilgrims arrived in what is now Plymouth, Massachusetts, in 1620, they were not the first Europeans to step foot on the mainland of North America. John Cabot landed in North America as early as 1497, and Giovanni da Verrazano traveled there in 1524. Just a few years before the Pilgrims, Samuel de Champlain (1605) and John Smith (1614) explored present-day New England. All these Europeans, and others too, brought with them diseases that killed as much as 75 percent of the Native American coastal population.

At the time the Pilgrims arrived, the Wampanoag were recovering from an epidemic that had killed 11,000 people, more than half their population. English explorers had also kidnapped Native Americans in New England, sometimes selling them into slavery. The Wampanoag had every reason to be suspicious of the new settlers, and Massasoit sent scouts to watch them from a distance.

The Wampanoag, however, needed an ally against their powerful neighbors, the Narragansett, who were untouched by the epidemic. Massasoit had his scouts observe the Pilgrims throughout their first winter, when

Massasoit

more than half the Plymouth settlers died. In the spring, perhaps realizing that the Pilgrims were too weak to threaten his tribe, Massasoit decided to befriend them. With his translator Squanto (see no. 2) interpreting, he negotiated a peace and friendship treaty with the Pilgrims. The pact called for mutual defense in case either people was attacked by a third party.

Massasoit's tribe taught the colonists how to plant and cook native crops. Without this help, the colony might not have survived. In the fall, Massasoit and sixty or more people from his tribe came to Plymouth for the first Thanksgiving feast. They brought five deer for the meal, which also included wild turkeys, geese, ducks, eels, shellfish, corn bread, succotash, squash, wild plums, and maple sugar.

The alliance between the Pilgrims and the Wampanoag was tested many times. As more colonists arrived in Massachusetts, land disputes arose. Sometimes the disputes resulted from cultural misunderstandings. The English sometimes thought they had purchased land outright, when Native Americans had only intended to share the right to use the land. Other times, newly arrived settlers simply moved onto Native American land without permission. Some English settlers raided Native American communities to get food.

Massasoit lost much of his respect for the English over the years, but he worked hard to maintain peace with them. He kept his treaty with the Pilgrims until his death in 1661.

4. Pocahontas
(c. 1595–1617)

Pocahontas was a force for peace between her people and the first English settlers at Jamestown. She was the daughter of Powhatan, the leader of the Powhatan confederacy, a league of thirty Algonquian tribes in present-day eastern Virginia. She was born just after the Native Americans in the area had been decimated by epidemics of European diseases, such as measles, bubonic plague, and typhus.

Despite the epidemics, the Powhatan were better off than the Jamestown community, which was established in 1607. The Native Americans were efficient farmers and grew plenty of beans, pumpkins, and corn. During the winter of 1608, when the English colonists began to starve because they hadn't planted sufficient crops, Pocahontas brought them food. Legend has it that around this time, Pocahontas also convinced her father to spare the life of English captain John Smith, whom the Native Americans had captured. Some historians, however, believe that Smith made up this story.

Pocahontas traveled freely among the Powhatan villages and the English settlements, and she sometimes negotiated with settlers on behalf of her father. When Pocahontas was thirteen, John Smith took seven hostages after a skirmish between the Powhatan and the colonists. Representing her father, Pocahontas successfully negotiated for the hostages' release.

In 1609, relations between the Native Americans and the English settlers broke down, and Powhatan planned to attack John Smith's camp. Pocahontas warned Smith, and he and his men were able to escape. The Powhatan, however, would no longer trade with or assist the Jamestown settlers.

In 1610, when Pocahontas was about fifteen, she married Kocoum, one of her father's allies, and went to live with the Patawamake on the Potomac River. In 1612, Samuel Argall, a Jamestown colonist and sea captain, visited the Patawamake and kidnapped Pocahontas. Argall hoped that if he held Pocahontas as a hostage, he could persuade Powhatan to release English hostages, guns, swords, and tools.

Pocahontas lived in Jamestown for a year. While she was being held captive, she converted to Christianity and took the name Rebecca. She also met John Rolfe, a businessman who had come to Jamestown to grow tobacco. The two fell in love and married in 1614, a move that helped bring about peace between the settlers and the Powhatan. (History does not record what happened to Pocahontas's first husband, Kocoum.) The next few years became known as the "Peace of Pocahontas," and it lasted for the rest of her short life.

In 1616, she traveled to England with her husband and their infant son, Thomas. In London, she was presented to King James I and his queen, who were impressed by her manner and appearance. Pocahontas died of an illness in 1617, just before she and her family were to return home to Virginia.

Pocahontas

Metacomet

Metacomet, the son of Massasoit (see no. 3), led Native American resistance against the English colonists in one of the bloodiest wars in early American history. The colonists called Metacomet "Philip," and this conflict is usually called "King Philip's War."

By the time of Massasoit's death in 1661, the balance of power in New England had shifted. Tens of thousands of English settlers lived in the region. The colonists were no longer dependent on Native Americans for their survival, as they were when Plymouth Colony was first founded. Beginning in the 1640s, waves of settlers had pressed farther and farther onto Native American land, and English cattle trampled Native American cornfields. In addition, colonial leaders tried to enforce English laws over tribes in their region.

When Metacomet became the leader of the Wampanoag, he tried to preserve the peace that his father had kept for more than forty years. Metacomet, however, was only maintaining peace to buy some time. He was working to develop a military alliance of New England tribes that, he hoped, could drive the English settlers out of New England. He is said to have declared, "I am determined not to live until I have no country." He meant that he would rather die fighting than live to see the day when Europeans would finally take all of the Wampanoag's land from them.

King Philip's War began in 1675. The Abenaki, Nipmuc, Pocumtuck, and Narraganset tribes all joined the Wampanoag as allies. The Narraganset went to war only after the colonists attacked them and killed several hundred men, women, and children. The fourteen months of war brought tremendous suffering to both settlers and Native Americans. Whole towns and villages were destroyed. Six hundred colonists and three thousand Native Americans, including almost all the Narraganset, were killed. At first, it seemed as if the Native Americans might actually drive the English from the continent. As time passed, however, Native American forces began to starve. Their crops were burned and the constant movements of the war gave them no time to plant new ones.

In 1676, a colonial force ambushed Metacomet in a swamp and killed him. The colonists beheaded and quartered his body and placed his head on a stake in Plymouth, where it was displayed for years. The war was basically over. So many Native Americans had died in the conflict that colonist Increase Mather wrote that it was "no unusual thing for those that traverse the woods to find dead Indians up and down ..." Many Native Americans fled the area, while the English sold many others into slavery in the West Indies.

Popé led one of the most successful revolts in Native American history. He and his allies drove the Spanish out of the area around Santa Fe, in present-day New Mexico, temporarily restoring the Pueblo's traditional way of life.

After the Spanish colonized New Mexico in 1598, they attempted to destroy the traditional Pueblo religion and to convert the Pueblo to Catholicism by force. The Pueblo continued to practice their religion secretly, in underground rooms called kivas. Spanish missionaries burned whatever kivas they could find and destroyed sacred religious objects, such as masks. When the Spanish caught the Pueblos practicing their religion, they treated them brutally. The Pueblo were often flogged in public. Sometimes, the Spanish even executed those who refused to convert. At other times, the Spanish cut off the hands or feet of nonbelievers or sold them into slavery.

While there are no details concerning Popé's early life, it is known that by the 1670s, he had become an important spiritual leader for the San Juan Pueblo. He was whipped at least three times for refusing to become a Christian, and he proudly exhibited the resulting scars on his back. Popé made no secret of his opposition to Spanish rule.

In 1675, the Spanish seized Popé and forty-six other Pueblo religious leaders. They took the prisoners to Santa Fe, where they hanged three and whipped and jailed the rest. After his release, Popé hid at the Taos Pueblo and planned a rebellion. He convinced many Pueblo leaders throughout the Southwest to join his conspiracy.

The attack took place on August 10, 1680, catching the Spanish by surprise. After ten days of fighting, the Pueblo forced the Spanish to retreat to El Paso. Popé took control of Pueblo life. He insisted that all Spanish churches and property be destroyed. He forbade the Pueblo to speak Spanish, and he required Christian Pueblos to purify themselves by bathing in suds of the yucca plant.

As time passed, Popé became a tyrannical leader. He executed people who disagreed with him. Popé was removed from office, but then he was reelected. At the same time, droughts were making life harder for the Pueblo community, and Popé's political alliance began to fall apart.

Popé died in 1690. Two years later, the Spanish reconquered the Santa Fe area. The revolt Popé led, however, had two lasting effects. When the Spanish retreated from Santa Fe, they left behind horses. The horses reproduced, and their offspring were traded to northern Native American groups. By the mid-1700s, horses had become indispensable to Native Americans living on the Great Plains. In addition, when the Spanish returned to Santa Fe, they did not outlaw the Pueblo traditional religion, which has survived to this day.

Pueblo in Taos, New Mexico

13

Kateri Tekakwitha

Kateri Tekakwitha, Lily of the Mohawks, is the first Native American to be beatified, or granted sainthood, by the Catholic Church.

Tekakwitha's Algonquin mother converted to Christianity before being kidnapped by a Mohawk chief, who became Tekakwitha's father. When Tekakwitha was four years old, a smallpox epidemic killed her parents and little brother. Tekakwitha barely survived. She lost most of her eyesight and was left with facial scars. She was adopted by her uncle, an important Mohawk leader who hated Christians, especially the Jesuits. In fact, the Mohawks tortured and killed several Jesuits in the years before Tekakwitha was born.

When Tekakwitha was a young girl, three priests visited her village, staying for three days. Tekakwitha listened to their teachings and, at age twenty, was baptized and became a Christian. She also decided to remain a virgin. From then on, her fellow Mohawks taunted her for refusing to work on Sundays and for refusing to marry. Some Mohawks felt that she was trying to avoid the responsibilities of a married Mohawk woman. Some also threw rocks at Tekakwitha, and her own family withheld food from her.

Eventually, Tekakwitha began receiving death threats and fled her village. She traveled by canoe to the Catholic mission at Kahnawake. There, she asked the Jesuits for permission to start her own convent. Although the priests were impressed with her piety, they felt she was too recent a convert for such a commitment. Tekakwitha took a vow of chastity, and she began to subject herself to rigorous physical trials to prove her faith. She ate very little food and mixed ashes into the food she did eat. Scantily clothed, she prayed outside in the middle of winter. She also slept on a bed of thorns and flogged herself with a whip.

Tekakwitha's behavior was so extreme that it alarmed the Jesuits. Among the Mohawks, people who could endure torture without showing their feelings were greatly respected, and Tekakwitha may have been trying to show that she was worthy of this kind of respect. Such practices destroyed her health, however, and she died at the age of twenty-four.

In 1943, she was declared venerable, the first step toward sainthood, by Pope Pius XII. To be beatified as a saint, a candidate must have shown "heroic virtue." Tekakwitha's virtue consisted of refusing to give up her faith even when it was dangerous to practice it, and living in a community where her faith made her subject to abuse, stoning, and death threats. Catholics consider her actions heroic because they were motivated by faith without concern for her well-being. Pope John Paul II beatified Kateri Tekakwitha in 1980 in Rome.

8. Pontiac
(c. 1720–1769)

The Ottawa chief Pontiac led one of the most important Native American military alliances in North American history.

Pontiac was born about 1720 and was raised as a traditional Ottawa. As a young boy, he learned about the history of his nation, and he also learned how to hunt and fight.

During Pontiac's youth, the Ottawa traded furs to French traders for guns and bullets. They lived in relative peace with French settlers in the Great Lakes region, where France's policy was to recognize Native American self-rule, territorial rights, and hunting and fishing rights. In 1763, however, France lost the Seven Years War and gave up much of its territory to Britain. The British rejected Native American land claims and allowed settlers to squat on Ottawa lands. These settlers tried to avoid trading guns and bullets to the Ottawa, who had grown to rely on the weapons.

The Ottawa nation had a democratic government. Each village had several chiefs who could lead only as long as they retained the respect of the people. Pontiac had become respected for his success in battle. He quickly gained enough influence to build alliances with other Native American nations. As the Ottawa and other nations grew more unhappy with the British, Pontiac devised a plan.

Pontiac's hope was that Native American nations could unite and, with help from France, force the British out of the Great Lakes region. He sent messages to nations from Lake Ontario all the way to the Mississippi River and planned a massive surprise attack on British forts in the region. The Seneca, Delaware, Shawnee, Miami, Ojibwa, and Missisauga all joined his alliance.

In 1763, Pontiac attacked the British fort at Detroit, but the British had been warned and the attack failed. Elsewhere, though, Pontiac's allies took over nine British forts and caused one other fort to be deserted. Only the Detroit fort and Fort Pitt, Pennsylvania, remained under British control.

At this point, the British began smuggling smallpox-infected blankets into Native American camps, producing an epidemic among the Delaware, Mingo, and Shawnee. Meanwhile, the allies learned that the war was damaging the fur trade in the Great Lakes area. Finally, Pontiac learned that the French, who he had hoped would join him, had signed a peace treaty with the British in London.

Pontiac ended the siege of Detroit, and the alliance began to break up. He signed a peace treaty with the British in 1765. A few years later, he was stabbed to death while on a trading trip to Cahokia, in present-day Illinois. Historians believe that Pontiac's alliance was the last time Native Americans had a real chance of stopping the westward expansion of European settlements.

Chief Pontiac speaking to tribes

9. Handsome Lake
(c. 1735–1815)

Handsome Lake, who was also known as Sedwa'gowa'ne (Our Great Teacher), founded the Longhouse religion that is still practiced by many Iroquois today. He also helped the Iroquois find a way to adapt to the tumultuous changes that occurred in their world during his lifetime.

When Handsome Lake was born, the Seneca nation was the largest and most important member of the Iroquois League. During the French and Indian Wars and the American Revolution, the Seneca sided with Great Britain. Handsome Lake fought in both wars. During the Revolution, colonial militias destroyed Seneca villages, and in 1797, when Handsome Lake was in his sixties, the United States moved the Seneca onto reservations. At the time, Handsome Lake was depressed and in the middle of a four-year drinking binge. By 1799, alcohol poisoning had turned his skin yellow. One day, he was found unconscious. His daughter, believing he was dead, called her family to the house to prepare his body for burial, but Handsome Lake was still alive. He was in a trance, experiencing a series of visions.

In Handsome Lake's visions, spiritual messengers gave him instructions for how to cure himself and Seneca society. When he recovered, he stopped drinking alcohol and began to preach a message called *Gaiwiio* (Good Word). Handsome Lake continued to have visions, and in his teachings, he combined traditional Seneca ideas with the message of Quaker missionaries.

He called for strict observance of Seneca religious ceremonies and emphasized values such as family, community, and the importance of land. Handsome Lake encouraged his followers to change their land use patterns in response to changing circumstances, by giving up hunting and becoming farmers. He also advocated abstention from drinking alcohol or practicing witchcraft. These teachings spread among the Iroquois and eventually developed into the Longhouse religion.

Handsome Lake's teachings, especially his views on giving up hunting for agriculture, drew opposition from other powerful leaders, particularly a chief named Red Jacket. Still, in 1801, Handsome Lake was elected a political leader of the Seneca. In 1802, he met with U.S. president Thomas Jefferson. He tried to persuade Jefferson to guarantee the Seneca their land and to stop traders from taking liquor onto the reservations.

A few years later, many of Handsome Lake's followers left him because he persecuted suspected witches. He became popular again in 1812, and he persuaded many Iroquois not to fight in the War of 1812.

Handsome Lake's teachings reached their greatest popularity many years after his death, in 1815. His followers published the *Code of Handsome Lake*, based partly on his teachings and partly on Quaker philosophy, in 1850. By the late twentieth century, about one third of the Iroquois living in New York State had become followers of the Longhouse religion.

Red Jacket

Molly Brant is believed to have been the most powerful Native American woman of the late 1700s. The sister of Mohawk leader Joseph Brant (see no. 12), she was born in a Mohawk village in present-day eastern New York State and grew up in a world that was filled with European influences. Her parents were Anglican Christians, and because she read and wrote English, historians believe she may have attended an English school as a child.

When Brant was in her early twenties, she married William Johnson, the British superintendent of Indian Affairs for the northern colonies. The marriage was a Mohawk ceremony, not recognized by the British, but it was important in cementing the military alliance between the British and some Iroquois nations.

Brant arranged for her younger brother Joseph to attend the school that later became Dartmouth College, and Joseph fought alongside Brant's husband Johnson during the French and Indian Wars and Pontiac's (see no. 8) Rebellion. Joseph later led the Mohawks and other Iroquois nations to support the British during the American Revolution. Molly bore eight or nine children to Johnson, managed his estate, and may have managed the Office of Indian Affairs in her husband's absence. When Johnson died in 1774, Molly was turned away from his estate, but she remained a British Loyalist.

When the American Revolution began, Brant became a spy for the British. Like many Mohawks, including her brother Joseph, she believed that Native Americans had a better chance of keeping at least some of their land if colonial expansion could be stopped. Brant was a persuasive voice within the Iroquois nation, and her influence is believed to have been as important as that of her brother Joseph in convincing some Iroquois tribes to side

Molly Brant

with the British in the war. In fact, George Washington once wrote of her, "I am afraid her influence will give us some trouble."

She provided the British with information about movements of colonial troops in the Mohawk Valley, and she carried ammunition to the British before the Battle of Oriskany in 1777. Because of her actions, colonial soldiers and their Oneida allies destroyed her house. Brant fled to Fort Niagara, where she continued her intelligence activities.

After the war ended, she moved to Ontario, Canada, with other Mohawk Loyalists. In recognition of her efforts during the war, Britain awarded her an annual pension of one hundred pounds—larger than the pension given to her brother Joseph, who had been an officer in the British army. She died in 1796, when she was about sixty years old.

Nanye'hi

Nanye'hi became a legendary warrior and diplomatic negotiator between the Cherokee and European settlers. She earned the highest honor available to a Cherokee woman in her day, the title of Beloved Woman, when she was only seventeen years old.

She was born in about 1738, and she distinguished herself very early in life. As a teenager, Nanye'hi married a Cherokee warrior named Kingfisher and had two children. Kingfisher fought in several wars between the Cherokee and the Creek, and Nanye'hi was usually at his side, loading his musket. In 1755, she and Kingfisher fought against the Creek in the Battle of Taliwa. During the battle, Kingfisher was shot and killed. Nanye'hi grabbed his musket and continued firing, singing a Cherokee war song. The Cherokee rallied and won the battle.

The Cherokee believed that they could not have won the Battle of Taliwa without Nanye'hi, and they gave her the title Beloved Woman. Cherokee Beloved Women played a complementary role to that of the peace and war chiefs, who were known as Beloved Men. As a Beloved Woman, she was the leader of the women's council of clan representatives and a member of the tribal council of chiefs.

In 1776, as the American Revolution was breaking out, the Cherokee sided with the British, and they planned a raid on settlements in the Holston and Wautauga Valleys. By then, Nanye'hi was married to an Irish trader named Brian Ward and had a child with him, and she was known as Nancy Ward. Nanye'hi disapproved of the raid. She warned the settlers, and most of them escaped.

After the colonists won their independence, Nanye'hi encouraged white settlers and Cherokee chiefs to negotiate their differences instead of fighting. She traveled tirelessly between Cherokee and white communities, even though American leaders occasionally objected to negotiating with a woman. In 1785, Nanye'hi helped to negotiate the Treaty of Hopewell, the first treaty between the Cherokee and the new United States.

Unfortunately, the United States did not respect its treaties with the Cherokee nation. In 1808 and 1817, Nanye'hi and the rest of the women's council urged the Cherokee to stop selling land to settlers, fearing that eventually the Americans would take over all the Cherokee lands. Then, the tribal council sold Nanye'hi's home village. Forced to move, Nanye'hi opened an inn on the Ocowee River, near present-day Benton, Tennessee.

Nanye'hi died about 1822. She did not live to see her fears realized with the Cherokee migration west in 1835, known as the "Trail of Tears." Nanye'hi is still a legend among the Cherokee, and the Chattanooga, Tennessee, chapter of the Daughters of the American Revolution is named after her.

12. Joseph Brant
(1742–1807)

Joseph Brant

Joseph Brant, also known as Thayendanegea, was a Mohawk chief who persuaded many warriors of the Iroquois Confederacy to fight for the British during the American Revolutionary War. After the war, he led them to Canada, where many of their descendants still live today.

Like his sister Molly (see no. 10), Joseph Brant grew up in two worlds, one traditionally Mohawk and one British. After Molly married William Johnson, a British official, she sent for her brother. When Joseph was nineteen, she arranged for him to attend Moor's Charity School for Indians, which later became Dartmouth College. There, he learned English so well that he became an interpreter and began translating the Bible into Mohawk. He also wrote several religious books, including a history of the Bible.

At the time, however, Brant's world was in turmoil, and he was not free to devote himself to religious studies. At the age of thirteen,

he had served in the British military with Molly's husband, William Johnson, during the French and Indian War. At age seventeen, he had served with Johnson's troops again. When he was twenty-one, Molly sent for him to come home. Brant returned to military service, this time leading a troop of Mohawk and Oneida volunteers against Pontiac (see no. 8) during Pontiac's Rebellion. After the war, Brant became an interpreter for the British Office of Indian Affairs.

In 1775, the British presented Brant with a captain's commission. He traveled to England and met King George III. When he returned, he began organizing the Iroquois to support the British during the American Revolution. He convinced most of the Mohawks, Senecas, Cayugas, and Onondagas. The Oneidas and the Tuscaroras, however, supported the revolutionaries, and the Iroquois League was fractured for the first time in hundreds of years.

Brant's troops fought at Cherry Valley, Minisink, and the Battle of Oriskany, as well as others. The American revolutionaries called Brant "Monster Brant" because of his ferocity as a warrior, but they were equally ferocious, destroying approximately forty Native American villages, along with hundreds of acres of farmland.

When the war ended, Brant and many other Mohawks moved to Ontario, Canada. The British gave Brant—by then a commissioned colonel—a pension equal to half his pay. In 1784, he arranged for Britain to grant the Iroquois some land on the Grand River in Ontario. Today, this area is known as the Six Nations Reserve. There, Brant raised his nine children and completed his translations of the Book of Common Prayer and the Gospel of Mark into Mohawk. Later in life, he traveled to the United States, meeting with President George Washington and speaking on behalf of peace along the American frontier.

Sequoyah

Sequoyah created a system of writing for the Cherokee language that became universally adopted by the entire Cherokee Nation.

Born about 1765, Sequoyah had a difficult childhood. Half Cherokee and half white, he grew up without a father and was labeled "half-breed." He never attended school and never learned to read or write English. As a child, Sequoyah did not play with other children, preferring to sit by himself and draw. He had been injured on a hunting trip and one leg was permanently disabled.

During the Creek War of 1813-1814, many Cherokee enlisted in the U.S. Army to fight their old enemy, the Creek. Sequoyah enlisted as well. In the army, Sequoyah was impressed with the usefulness of writing symbols on paper to communicate meaning. He became determined to create a system of writing for the Cherokee.

Sequoyah worked on his project for twelve years. His family and friends thought that his idea was foolish. Some Cherokees even thought Sequoyah might be practicing some form of witchcraft. More than once, they burned his work. Once, they burned his entire cabin.

Sequoyah pressed on, however, finally detecting eighty-six separate sounds in the Cherokee language. To communicate these sounds, he borrowed letters from English, Greek, and Hebrew, and he created some new letters himself. He also extended the Cherokee system of numbers, inventing a system of arithmetic that would express numbers up to one million. Then, Sequoyah taught his six-year-old daughter, Ah-yoka, to read and write.

In 1821, Sequoyah and Ah-yoka presented his work to the Eastern Cherokee Tribal Council. During the next year, Sequoyah taught thousands of Cherokee to read and write, refusing to accept payment for his teaching. The Cherokee had become the first Native American tribe north of Mexico to have its own system of writing. In 1824, the Eastern Cherokee Nation gratefully awarded Sequoyah a silver medal and a lifetime pension for his work. Then, Sequoyah moved to Arkansas, where he taught his system to the Western Cherokee.

In 1828, the Cherokee Tribal Council began to print a newspaper using Sequoyah's system. Soon, a tribal constitution was written down. Sequoyah became the president of the western branch of the Cherokee.

In 1838, U.S. president Andrew Jackson illegally forced the Eastern Cherokee to move west in a winter march that became known as the "Trail of Tears." When the Eastern Cherokee arrived, Sequoyah helped the two branches of Cherokee work together to create one government for the Cherokee Nation. Sequoyah died in 1843.

Black Hawk led the Sauk and Fox resistance to white settlers who claimed the Native Americans' lands. The conflict became known as the Black Hawk War.

He was born in the Sauk summer village that later became Rock Island, Illinois. The Sauk farmed there in the summer and moved west to mine lead and hunt in the winter. Black Hawk became a warrior and, by his late teens, was leading war parties.

In 1804, southern Sauk and Mesquakie leaders signed the Treaty of St. Louis, turning 50,000,000 acres (20,235,000 ha) of land—all tribal land east of the Mississippi, including Black Hawk's home—over to the United States. Black Hawk believed that the leaders who signed the treaty had been intoxicated by alcohol that U.S. negotiator William Henry Harrison had offered them. Black Hawk also claimed that southern leaders could not represent the northern branches of the Sauk and Mesquakie. The leaders themselves thought that they had only given the United States the right to share their hunting grounds. They soon learned, however, that the U.S. government claimed to own the land.

Along with Tecumseh (see no. 15), Black Hawk and the Sauk fought against the United States in the War of 1812. The British told the Native Americans that the war would not end until their land was returned to them. Instead, Britain made a peace with the United States that left the 1804 treaty in place. Black Hawk's rival, Keokuk, agreed to abide by the treaty, and moved a group of Mesquakie to Iowa. Black Hawk, however, stayed in Illinois.

In 1829, Black Hawk and his band returned from their winter hunt to find U.S. settlers living in their lodges and plowing their fields. The Sauk stayed, sharing their village with the settlers. In 1831, the U.S. government forced the Sauk into Iowa. They returned the next year to plant their corn as usual, knowing that

Black Hawk

this time they would have to resist the U.S. military. Black Hawk may have expected help from the British, as well as the Winnebagos and the Potawatomis, but all three parties remained neutral.

On May 14, Black Hawk sent messengers with a flag of truce toward the U.S. troops, but nervous militiamen fired on them. The Sauk won the ensuing battle and then fled into present-day Wisconsin. Black Hawk tried to persuade his followers to march further north, and about fifty left with him. The next day, U.S. troops massacred the remaining three hundred, including elders and children. Black Hawk was captured and imprisoned. The following year, he was released.

For a time, Black Hawk toured the country, telling his story. His defeat allowed the complete white settlement of what had been the Old Northwest territory.

Shawnee leader Tecumseh led a confederacy of Native American nations. He fought alongside the British against the United States in the War of 1812.

Born near present-day Springfield, Ohio, Tecumseh had a tumultuous upbringing. When he was a child, settlers began to arrive in the Ohio Valley, illegally squatting on Native American land. When he was only about six, his father was killed by settlers. A year later, his mother moved to present-day Missouri, leaving Tecumseh to be raised by his sister and brother. Within a few years, Cornstalk, a great Shawnee leader and mentor to Tecumseh, was murdered by settlers. In years to come, Tecumseh was to see two of his brothers killed in battles against the United States.

Tecumseh came of age during the Revolutionary War, fighting with the British against the colonists. Afterward, he continued to fight against settlers along the frontier, but he earned a reputation for treating prisoners of war humanely.

After 1790, waves of settlers moved into the Ohio Valley. During this time, some Native Americans sold the United States large areas of land that they did not own. Tecumseh spoke out against this practice and refused to recognize treaties such as the Treaty of Greenville (1795), in which Native Americans gave up claims to southern, central, and eastern Ohio. Tecumseh believed that the land belonged collectively to all Native Americans and could not be sold by a few without the consent of all. Despite his disagreements with the United States, he sometimes agreed to negotiate on the U.S. government's behalf, speaking eloquently to calm panicky settlers and to prevent violent conflicts along the frontier.

About 1808, Tecumseh moved to present-day Indiana, and he began to organize a confederacy of Native American nations. He traveled as far away as New York and Florida, rallying thousands of Native Americans to join his confederacy. Tecumseh's momentum was lost in 1811, however, when his brother Tenskwatawa—who had become a powerful Shawnee religious leader called the Prophet—ordered an attack upon William Henry Harrison's troops while Tecumseh was away. The U.S. troops won the battle and destroyed the village of Tippecanoe.

In 1812, realizing that war was about to break out between the United States and Great Britain, Tecumseh and his followers—more than one thousand warriors—joined a British army in Canada. Tecumseh took command of a troop of British and Native American soldiers, earning the rank of brigadier general in the British army. In August 1812, he helped capture Detroit and 2,500 U.S. soldiers. By October, however, Britain began to suffer setbacks, and during the retreat of British troops into Canada, Tecumseh was killed at the Battle of the Thames. Soon after Tecumseh's death, his confederacy dissolved.

Tecumseh

22

Kennekuk
(c. 1785–1852)

Some Native American leaders resisted the westward expansion of the United States by putting up a physical fight. Others found non-violent methods of resistance. Kennekuk, the leader of the Vermillion, the northern branch of the Kickapoo, was one such person.

Traditionally, the Kickapoo were a wandering, hunting-gathering people. As the United States expanded westward, the government encouraged Native Americans to become farmers. Many Native American economies were already based on farming. Kennekuk knew that white settlers would feel less threatened by a community of Native Americans who were peaceful farmers. Hoping that the Kickapoo would be able to coexist with the settlers and keep their land, he encouraged his followers to take up farming. They did, and the U.S. government helped subsidize the farms that he established.

Kennekuk was not just a political leader, but a religious one, too. At the same time that he pushed the Kickapoo to transform their economy, he also taught his followers to adhere to their traditional religious beliefs. After experiencing an intense religious vision, Kennekuk taught the Kickapoo to fast and meditate regularly. He also spoke out against violent behavior and the consumption of alcohol.

His strategy for keeping Kickapoo lands worked, but only for a while. The Kickapoo prospered as farmers, and settlers coveted their fields. During the 1820s, the famous explorer William Clark, who was then superintendent of Indian Affairs in St. Louis, met often with Kennekuk, urging him to sign a treaty to give up the land and agree to move elsewhere.

At first Kennekuk refused. Then, he began to use passive resistance to delay the relocation of his people. He met frequently with government officials, telling them that the Kickapoo had decided to move but were not ready yet. He offered a variety of excuses, such as having

Kennekuk

to harvest crops or illness in the community, for the delays. In this way he was able to postpone the move for more than ten years.

After the Black Hawk (see no. 14) War in 1832, settlers were nervous about living so close to a Native American community, even a peaceful one. The government finally forced Kennekuk to sign a treaty agreeing to relocate to Kansas. Even after signing the treaty, Kennekuk managed to delay the move, but he and his band finally relocated in 1833.

In the years to come, Kennekuk continued to use his skills as a shrewd negotiator to benefit the Kickapoo. He also continued to teach his traditional religion. Kennekuk caught smallpox and died in 1852, just as the government began pressuring the Kickapoo to give up more land. His band of the Kickapoo grew smaller, until eventually its last members died.

Sacajawea

Sacajawea served as a guide and interpreter for American explorers Meriwether Lewis and William Clark, on their historic journey to explore the newly acquired territory of the Louisiana Purchase in the early 1800s.

Many specific details of Sacajawea's life are unknown. A member of the Shoshone, she was probably born in the late 1780s in present-day central Idaho. When Sacajawea was about twelve, Hidatsa warriors attacked her family's camp, killing eight adults and kidnapping Sacajawea and several other children. Between 1800 and 1804, Sacajawea and another girl were either sold to, or won in a gambling match by, a French-Canadian trader named Toussaint Charbonneau. Later, Charbonneau married both girls.

In October 1804, Lewis and Clark's expedition arrived at Sacajawea's village in present-day North Dakota. The explorers built cabins and decided to stay for the winter. When Charbonneau learned about the expedition, he offered the services of himself and Sacajawea as interpreters for the trip. Lewis and

Clark accepted the offer, although Sacajawea was pregnant. She gave birth to a son, Jean-Baptiste, in February, and she carried him on her back in a cradle board when the expedition headed west in the spring.

The lone female member of the forty-man expedition, Sacajawea made invaluable contributions on the journey west. She interpreted for the explorers as they encountered various tribes, and she provided expert guidance through present-day Montana. She also gathered edible plants for everyone to eat, and on one occasion, she saved their journals, instruments, and medicine after Charbonneau accidentally capsized one of the boats.

In midsummer, the party entered Shoshone territory, where Sacajawea was reunited with her brother, who had become the Shoshone leader. At her request, he provided horses, supplies, and guides to help the explorers make their way across the Rocky Mountains. After navigating the Clearwater, Snake, and Columbia Rivers, the party reached the Pacific Ocean in November 1805.

When the expedition returned to Sacajawea's village in 1806, Clark offered to adopt her son Jean-Baptiste. Charbonneau and Sacajawea refused the offer, but sometime later, they traveled to St. Louis to leave Jean-Baptiste with Clark so he could receive a Western education. Clark later adopted Jean-Baptiste as his own, believing that Sacajawea was dead.

Historians are uncertain when Sacajawea died. Some believe, as Clark did, that she died at age twenty-five of a fever. Others believe that it was Charbonneau's other wife who died of the fever. According to Shoshone oral tradition, Sacajawea married a Comanche man, had five more children, became an important political leader, and lived to be one hundred. In addition to numerous memorials along the explorers' route, Sacajawea also has a river, a mountain, and a pass named in her honor.

18. Seathl
(c. 1788–1866)

Seathl, the Native American for whom the city of Seattle is named, is often regarded as the last great Native American leader of the Pacific Northwest.

The principal chief of the Duwamish, Suquamish, and allied nations, Seathl was born near present-day Puget Sound in about 1788. He was about four years old when English navigator George Vancouver sailed into the Sound, hoping to find a route through the continent to Hudson Bay. Vancouver met with the Duwamish and Suquamish, but after his visit, these Native Americans saw very few settlers from the United States and Canada for the next several decades.

During his early years, Seathl became a warrior, and he was respected for his fearlessness in battle. Meanwhile, more settlers moved west toward the Pacific. In 1833, the Hudson Bay Company built a trading post at the southern end of Puget Sound. During the 1830s, Catholic missionaries traveled to the region, and they converted Seathl to Christianity. From that time on, historians believe, Seathl was determined to coexist peacefully with the settlers that, he knew, would eventually be on their way. It wasn't until the early 1850s, however, that the first settlers arrived to establish what would later become the city of Seattle.

When the settlers did arrive, the Duwamish and Suquamish welcomed and helped them. The settlers wanted to honor Seathl for his help by naming their community "Seattle." Seathl objected. He believed that, after he was dead, his spirit would be disturbed if people said his name. Eventually, he persuaded the settlers to pay him a small tax to compensate him in advance for the disturbance to his spirit.

Although the Duwamish and Suquamish remained at peace with the settlers, other Pacific Northwest nations rebelled against the encroachments on their land. In 1855, territorial governor Isaac Stevens asked some nations to move onto reservations. Seathl and other leaders agreed, after insisting that some of their most prized lands be included as part of the reservations. Seathl was the first to sign the Port Elliott Treaty stipulating the boundaries of the reservations. Then, he gave an eloquent farewell address. Since at least four versions of the speech survive today, nobody is sure exactly what Seathl said, although he is often quoted. In one version, Seathl remarks, "How can you buy or sell the sky, the warmth of the land? The idea is strange to us."

Several Native American nations in the Pacific Northwest refused to accept the Port Elliott Treaty, and battles continued for more than fifteen years. Seathl refused to allow his community to go to war, and he ensured that his people lived in peace and safety on the reservation he had chosen for them.

Seathl

Mangas Coloradas united the Apache nation against the United States. For this reason, many historians consider Mangas to be the most important Apache leader of the nineteenth century.

Mangas's band lived in the Mimbres Mountains, in the south of present-day New Mexico. The region was part of Mexico, a colony of Spain. The Apaches had long considered Mexico to be their enemy, but during Mangas's youth, the two sides were at peace. They went to war again after Mexico won its independence from Spain, in 1821. By 1835, Apache warriors had killed five thousand Mexican settlers. Mexican leaders then placed a bounty on all Apache scalps.

A special bounty was placed on the head of the Mimbreño Apache leader Juan Jose Compas. In 1837, an American trapper who was a trusted friend of Compas arrived at Compas's camp with a band of armed men.

Mangas Coloradas

They killed Compas and twenty other Apaches to obtain the reward money. After Compas's death, Mangas Coloradas became the leader of the Mimbreño. He began a series of raids against the Mexicans that would eventually make his name, as one historian has remarked, "synonymous with terror."

Mangas also tried to bring about peace, sometimes risking his own life to do so. In 1846, he signed a peace treaty with the United States, which had taken possession of New Mexico after the Mexican War, and provided troops with safe passage through Apache territory. Then, in 1851, Anglo gold miners arrived in the Santa Rita mountains, angering the Apaches. Mangas approached the miners and offered to lead them to another area. The miners tied him to a tree and whipped him severely, as a warning, they said, "for Indians to stay away from whites."

In revenge, Mangas raided local settlements. In 1852, he and other leaders signed a peace treaty at Acoma, but the treaty was not ratified by the U.S. Congress, and the raids continued. The situation grew so bad that a U.S. Army report recommended giving New Mexico back to the Native Americans and to Mexico.

Mangas Coloradas arranged alliances between his band and several other Apache groups. He and another Apache leader, Cochise (see no. 26), became allies in 1861. They tried to drive all Anglo Americans out of Apache territory. They nearly succeeded, reducing the Anglo population of New Mexico and Arizona for several years.

In 1863, U.S. soldiers invited Mangas to negotiate a peace. He rode alone to Fort McClean, where he was captured. Brigadier General J.R. West told soldiers that he didn't want Mangas to be alive the next morning. The soldiers tortured and killed him. They later claimed he had been killed while trying to escape.

Osceola led Seminole resistance to the U.S. government during the 1830s, when it sought to relocate eastern Native American nations to lands west of the Mississippi River.

The Seminole nation was originally made up of Creeks who migrated to Florida from Georgia, as well as their African American slaves, fugitive slaves, and their descendants. Osceola was born in Georgia. After the Creek War, a civil war between two factions of Creek, Osceola and his mother moved to Florida.

Spain sold Florida to the United States in 1819, after the First Seminole War (1817–1819). In 1823, the U.S. government moved the Seminole to a Florida reservation. The land on the reservation was poor, but the Seminole lived there peacefully. Osceola worked as a guide and helped surveyors mark reservation boundaries. After a few years, the Seminole asked for a grant of swampland, and Osceola moved to the Everglades.

In 1830, the U.S. Congress passed the Indian Removal Act. The act authorized U.S. president Andrew Jackson to offer lands west of the Mississippi River to eastern Native American nations. The Chickasaw, Choctaw, Seminole, Cherokee, and Creeks resisted the move, and Jackson decided to use the military to evict them. As much as 25 percent of some groups died on these forced marches.

In 1832, the government decided to move the Seminole to Arkansas and reunite them with the Creeks, whom many Seminole had fought during the Creek War. A few Seminole leaders signed a treaty agreeing to the move, but other Seminoles were horrified, especially because the treaty required that Seminoles of African American descent be treated as runaway slaves. Osceola knew what it was like to lose a loved one to slave-catchers; his wife, the daughter of a fugitive slave, had been seized and shipped to the slave states. He began organizing resistance to the relocation.

Osceola

U.S. agent Wiley Thompson tried to force a new removal and relocation treaty on the Seminole in 1835. Most Seminole leaders refused to sign it, and Osceola slashed the treaty with his knife. Thompson imprisoned Osceola, who finally signed the treaty in order to be released. Then, he vanished into the Everglades, where many Seminole took their families to hide.

For two years, during the conflict known as the Second Seminole War (1835-1842), Osceola and his followers waged guerrilla warfare against the United States. The Seminole were outnumbered, but they managed to kill hundreds of U.S. soldiers. In 1837, Osceola met U.S. general Thomas Jesup under a truce flag, but Jesup arrested him. Osceola died of unknown causes in prison, in 1838.

Led by Billy Bowlegs (see no. 24) and others, the Seminole continued to resist relocation. Over the next five years, however, about 3,800 Seminoles were removed to Arkansas. A few hundred remained in the Everglades.

Black Kettle
(1804–1868)

Black Kettle

Black Kettle was a leader of the Southern Cheyenne. He struggled, unsuccessfully, to bring about peace between his community and the U.S. government at a time when tensions between settlers and Native Americans were extremely high.

As a young man, Black Kettle participated in wars against the Ute and Delaware, but he advocated for peace with the United States. In 1851, the Cheyenne signed the Treaty of Fort Laramie, which guaranteed them lands in western Kansas and eastern Colorado. During the 1859 gold rush, however, settlers rushed into the area, in violation of the treaty.

In 1861, Black Kettle signed a treaty agreeing to a reservation at Sand Creek, Colorado. The land there was not farmable, and the nearest buffalo herd was 200 miles (321 km) away. Black Kettle could not stop young Cheyenne warriors from raiding settlements and wagon trains, and state militias did not distinguish between peaceful and hostile Native Americans. Settlers were terrified, and newspapers called for the extermination of all Native Americans. Black Kettle visited Fort Weld, Colorado, to negotiate for peace, and he received permission to camp at Sand Creek during the negotiations.

Colorado's governor, however, had formed citizen militias who were authorized to kill any hostile Native Americans they could find. One militia, armed with howitzer cannons and led by Colonel John Chivington, approached Black Kettle's camp at dawn on November 29, 1864. Of the six hundred people in the camp, only about thirty-five were warriors. The rest were old men, women, and children.

Black Kettle raised the U.S. flag and a white flag to show his peaceful intentions, and junior officers riding with Chivington told him that these Cheyenne had given up their weapons and been promised army protection. Nevertheless, Chivington ordered his troops to attack. About two hundred Cheyenne, mostly women and children, were killed, and their bodies were mutilated.

Despite the massacre, Black Kettle continued to press for peace. He signed treaties in 1865 and 1867, and he led his community to reservations, first in Kansas and then in Oklahoma. He kept the peace, although some Cheyenne bands continued to make war. When fighting broke out in the fall of 1868, Black Kettle visited Fort Cobb to tell the commander that he wanted peace. Told that the only safe place for his people was the area around the fort, Black Kettle began preparing to move.

On the day Black Kettle's band was to leave, Colonel George Custer and the Seventh Cavalry attacked his camp, although it was flying a white flag. They killed Black Kettle and more than one hundred others, ninety-three of whom were old men, women, and children.

Washakie
(c. 1804–1900)

Washakie was an Eastern Shoshone leader who befriended Oregon Trail settlers and the U.S. Army during the mid-1800s. His insistence on peaceful coexistence with settlers helped him to bargain for a reservation on fertile land in traditional Shoshone territory, in present-day western Wyoming.

As a young man, Washakie fought in battles against the Blackfeet and Crows, earning a reputation as a courageous warrior. Throughout his life, he continued to fight Native American enemies of the Shoshone, while remaining at peace with the United States.

During the 1820s and 1830s, Washakie befriended the explorers, trappers, and traders who arrived in his territory. He became the principal leader of his community in the 1840s, when settlers were beginning to migrate along the Oregon Trail. He refused to allow Shoshone warriors to harm the settlers, even when settlers destroyed herds and lands that the Shoshone needed.

Washakie provided Shoshone warrior patrols to protect the immigrants from raids by the Sioux, Cheyenne, and Arapaho, enemies of the Shoshone. He also helped settlers to find lost cattle and to cross rivers safely. Nine thousand settlers signed a document commending Washakie and thanking him for his help.

In 1862, against Washakie's orders, a group of Shoshone joined the Bannock in raiding some wagon trains and settlements. Knowing there was a danger that settlers would try to punish his entire community for these acts, Washakie led the Eastern Shoshone to take refuge at Fort Bridger. They were reunited with the rest of the Shoshone in 1863. That year, Washakie signed a treaty guaranteeing safe passage to travelers.

In 1868, he agreed to settle the Eastern Shoshone on the Wind River Reservation. Washakie did not want to confine his people to a reservation. He made a practical decision, ensuring that his community would be able to remain in its homeland, safe from the massacres that were being suffered by so many other Native American nations.

Younger warriors sometimes criticized Washakie's cooperation with the U.S. government. When the government violated its treaty with the Shoshone in 1870, reducing the amount of land set aside for the reservation, some young warriors tried to remove Washakie as chief. Washakie, who was nearly seventy, left camp. He returned two months later with six scalps of Native American enemies of the Shoshone. His critics stopped complaining.

Throughout the rest of his life, Washakie continued to help the U.S. army, providing scouts to the U.S. government for its wars against the Arapaho, Cheyenne, Sioux, and Ute. When he died in 1900, Washakie was buried with full military honors at a fort the army named after him.

Washakie

23. Stand Watie
(1806–1871)

Stand Watie signed the treaty that agreed to the relocation of the Cherokee nation from Georgia to present-day Oklahoma. He later became a brigadier general in the Confederate army during the Civil War.

Watie was born in Georgia and educated at mission schools. When he returned home from school, he became a planter and also helped to publish the *Cherokee Phoenix* newspaper. At the time, the Cherokee nation was divided on the question of what to do about settlers taking their lands. Watie became a member of the "Treaty party," which advocated signing a treaty to give up land in Georgia in exchange for land in the west. Although not authorized to do so, Watie and other members of his party signed a treaty agreeing to the removal of the Cherokee and their resettlement in Oklahoma.

The lawful government of the Cherokee nation petitioned the U.S. Senate not to ratify the treaty and, after the Senate did so, contested the removal plans in the U.S. Supreme Court. The Cherokee won their case, but U.S. president Andrew Jackson forced them to move anyway.

In the meantime, Watie and his family had already moved to Oklahoma, along with other members of the Treaty party. Watie brought with him the slaves from his plantation, and he established a new plantation in his new home. The rest of the Cherokee were forced to march on the infamous "Trail of Tears" during the winter of 1838 to 1839, and thousands died along the way from hunger, cold, and exhaustion.

When the Eastern Cherokee arrived, they disagreed with the Western Cherokee—those Cherokee who, like Watie, had already moved west—about the form the new Cherokee government should take. All the Cherokee who had signed the removal treaty were killed except for Watie, who was warned and managed to escape. Over time, the Cherokee settled their differences. Watie served as a member of the Cherokee National Council for more than a decade, and he was its speaker for two years.

When the Civil War began, many members of the Cherokee nation supported the Confederacy. Some Cherokee owned slaves, and many wanted revenge against the Union for the Trail of Tears. Other Cherokees fought on the side of the Union. Watie organized a Cherokee regiment and was commissioned as a colonel in the Confederate army. In 1864, Watie was promoted to brigadier general, the only Native American to hold that rank in either army during the Civil War.

After the war, Watie helped negotiate the 1866 Cherokee Reconstruction Treaty. He died in 1871.

Stand Watie

Billy Bowlegs led the Seminole resistance to relocation in the Second and Third Seminole Wars. Bowlegs's group became one of the last bands to stay in Florida after the U.S. government had begun trying to relocate them.

Bowlegs was a young boy at the time of the First Seminole War (1817–1819). He became a chief of the Seminole at the age of twenty, in time to lead a group of guerrillas in the Second Seminole War (1835-1842). Bowlegs fought alongside Osceola (see no. 20) until Osceola was captured. Several Seminole leaders, including Osceola, were captured under truce flags and taken to Arkansas. As these leaders were removed, their followers began to surrender and move west.

By the end of the Second Seminole War, only a few hundred Seminoles remained in Florida. Billy Bowlegs and his followers were among them. Bowlegs agreed to a treaty that allotted some land in Florida to the remaining Seminoles. At the same time, Bowlegs continued to negotiate with the U.S. government about the possibility of relocating the rest of the Seminole community westward. Bowlegs did everything he could to prolong the negotiations, knowing that his people could live in peace while the matter was being settled.

In 1852, Bowlegs and other Seminole leaders met with U.S. president Millard Fillmore in Washington, D.C. The U.S. army hoped the trip would convince the Seminole leaders that the United States was too powerful to be resisted, but Bowlegs was determined not to leave his home.

In 1855, a group of army engineers and surveyors trampled some Seminole farmland, destroying crops and taking produce. Some historians believe the engineers were provoking Bowlegs on purpose to see what he would do. His response was to take up arms again, starting the Third Seminole War (1855-1858).

Billy Bowlegs

Bowlegs and his followers fought on, long after most of the remaining Seminole had surrendered and moved west. As he and his band grew short of supplies, the army sent a group of Arkansas Seminoles to persuade him to migrate west. Bowlegs agreed, but some of his followers did not. They remained in Florida, living in isolated parts of the Everglades. Today, their descendants are proud to say that they are the only Native American nation never to surrender to the United States.

Billy Bowlegs traveled to the Seminole reservation, but historians are not quite sure what became of him after the move. Some believe that he died of smallpox in 1859 or 1864, while others claim that he fought as a Union soldier in the Civil War and died in 1861.

Dull Knife was the co-leader of the Northern Cheyenne on their 1,500-mile (2,400-km) journey from their reservation in present-day Oklahoma back to their homeland in what is now Montana. The Cheyenne who survived the journey lived on a reservation in Montana's Rosebud Valley.

Dull Knife's actual name was Morning Star, but most people called him Dull Knife because his brother-in-law liked to joke that his knife was not sharp. As a young man, Dull Knife earned a reputation as a warrior and became a member of his tribal government. By the time he was in his sixties, he had become one of four chiefs who, according to Cheyenne tradition, stood for the four Sacred Persons who lived at the universe's cardinal points and guarded creation.

He joined Red Cloud's (see no. 29) band during Red Cloud's War in 1866, and he may have helped Crazy Horse (see no. 41) defeat Colonel George Custer at the Battle of the Little Bighorn. In 1876, an army force looking for Crazy Horse found Dull Knife's camp instead, and a battle ensued. During the battle, the entire camp—including shelters, clothing, blankets, and food—was destroyed. The survivors fled to Crazy Horse's camp, and eleven children froze to death on the journey.

Along with Crazy Horse, Dull Knife decided to surrender, and his community moved to a reservation in Oklahoma. The land was not suitable for farming or hunting, and there were malaria epidemics. Half of the Cheyenne died in the first year. Dull Knife and another Cheyenne chief, Little Wolf (see no. 28), asked to be relocated to the Great Plains, but the U.S. Army refused. In September 1878, Dull Knife and Little Wolf led a group of three hundred off the reservation and headed home, with ten thousand soldiers on their trail. In Nebraska, the two leaders split up.

Dull Knife's band was captured and taken to Fort Robinson. After refusing to return to Oklahoma, they were jailed in a freezing barracks, with no food or water, for three days. Finally, they tried to escape, making a run for it with their children under their arms and on their backs. Soldiers shot at them as they fled, killing twenty-two men, eight women, and two children. Most of the others were recaptured, but a few, including Dull Knife and some of his family members, escaped. They spent eighteen days walking to the Pine Ridge Reservation in South Dakota, subsisting on bark.

At that point, the U.S. government abandoned its efforts to relocate the Northern Cheyenne to Oklahoma, and it gave the surviving members of both Dull Knife's and Little Wolf's bands a reservation in their home territory in Montana. Dull Knife died there about 1883.

Dull Knife (right) with Little Wolf

26. Cochise
(c. 1812–1874)

Cochise, a leader of the Chiricahua Apache, led his people's resistance to Anglo settlement of the Southwest during the 1860s. A formidable warrior, he later became such a force for peace that, when he became deathly ill, even Anglo settlers feared the possible consequences of his demise.

Historians know very little about Cochise's early life. They do know that, as a young man, he occasionally helped American settlers. In 1858, Cochise agreed to guard stagecoaches passing through Apache territory. He was regarded throughout the region as a peaceful, fair, and honorable person. Then, in 1861, U.S. Army lieutenant George Bascom wrongly accused Cochise of having kidnapped an Anglo child. Bascom tried to arrest Cochise, but Cochise cut a hole in the side of his tent and escaped, despite being shot three times. Bascom arrested six other Apache warriors, so Cochise kidnapped three Anglos and attempted to organize a prisoner exchange. Bascom refused, and both sides killed their prisoners.

Cochise joined forces with Mangas Coloradas (see no. 19). Together, they drove Anglos out of present-day New Mexico and Arizona during the U.S. Civil War. After Mangas died in 1863, Cochise and his band terrorized Anglo settlements. U.S. general William Tecumseh Sherman remarked that the United States had fought one war with Mexico to get the Southwest and should fight another "to make her take it back."

Despite Cochise's reputation for cruelty during war, Anglos who approached his camp peacefully could be received peacefully. In 1871, the army changed its approach to the Apache wars, sending out scouts to locate and negotiate peace with individual bands of Apache, instead of trying to conquer them.

Meanwhile, a mail carrier named Thomas Jeffords, who had lost fourteen employees to Cochise's warriors, decided to pay Cochise a

Naiche, the second son of Cochise

visit. He walked up to Cochise's camp alone, and he offered his firearms in exchange for a talk. The two negotiated a deal, and from then on, Jeffords's mail carriers were allowed to pass safely through Cochise's territory.

In 1872, Jeffords also arranged a meeting between Cochise and U.S. general Oliver Howard, and Howard offered Cochise a reservation in New Mexico. Cochise considered the offer but warned Howard that many Apache would not be willing to go there. He promised General Howard that the Chiricahua Apache would stop fighting in return for a reservation in the Chiricahua Mountains. His people were given the reservation, and Cochise kept his promise all his life.

Unfortunately, the U.S. army did not realize Cochise could not speak for all the Apache, and it blamed him when some Apaches continued to wage war. The U.S. government decided to shut down the Chiricahua reservation and send the Apache to New Mexico, but Cochise died before the move occurred.

Manuelito was a major Navajo war leader. After the Navajo made their tragic "Long Walk," Manuelito helped persuade the U.S. government that they should have a reservation in their homeland.

In 1848, the United States ended its war with Mexico and annexed the Southwest as a new U.S. territory. In 1855, the same year that Manuelito became a chief in his community, the U.S. government built Fort Defiance, in present-day New Mexico, near an area the Navajo used as grazing land for their horses.

The post commander decided to use the area adjacent to the fort as grazing land for the fort's horses and ordered the Navajo to move their livestock. Manuelito defiantly refused, and one day, the army shot sixty of his horses and more than one hundred sheep. The situation escalated until the Navajo attacked Fort Defiance. The war lasted only a few weeks before a peace treaty was signed.

In 1861, U.S. troops began to leave the area to fight in the Civil War. Navajo chiefs Manuelito, Barboncito, and Herrero Grande saw a chance to drive the remaining soldiers away, and they persuaded between one and two thousand Navajo, Ute, Apache, and Pueblo to join them in attacking the fort. The fort's commander had been warned of the surprise attack, however, and the U.S. soldiers managed to drive the warriors back with cannons.

In 1863, General James Carleton began a massive effort to force the Navajo to relocate to Bosque Redondo, a reservation in New Mexico. He assigned Colonel Kit Carson to do the job. Knowing he could not defeat the Navajo militarily in their homeland, Carson began destroying Navajo homes, crops, and livestock. Forced to subsist on berries and wild nuts, the Navajo could not make it through the winter.

In February 1864, they began turning themselves in, to begin what became known as the Long Walk. More than two hundred Navajo died during this 350-mile (560-km) journey. Some died of hunger and cold, while others drowned in the Rio Grande, which they were forced to cross during the spring flood. When they arrived at Bosque Redondo, conditions were no better. More than two thousand Navajos died there of disease and starvation. The U.S. army removed General Carleton from command, and in 1868, Manuelito and other chiefs traveled to Washington, D.C., to negotiate for the Navajo's return home.

Although the government had planned to relocate the Navajo to present-day Oklahoma, Manuelito pleaded eloquently for the Navajo to return to their homeland. Finally, the government agreed to a 3.5 million-acre (1.4 million-ha) reservation in the Southwest.

From 1870 to 1885, Manuelito served as the principal chief of the Navajo nation. During Manuelito's time as chief, the Navajo rebuilt their communities, and many Navajo became prosperous ranchers.

Manuelito

As a strong advocate of peace and cooperation with the U.S. government, Little Wolf helped the Northern Cheyenne survive an arduous journey from their reservation in present-day Oklahoma back to their homeland in what is now Montana.

As a teenager, Little Wolf became known as a warrior. As American settlers began to arrive in Cheyenne native lands, however, Little Wolf advocated living peacefully with them. He broke the peace only once, attacking army troops in 1865 to avenge their 1864 massacre of Cheyenne at Sand Creek. Like Dull Knife (see no. 25), Little Wolf and his followers were attacked following the Battle of the Little Bighorn. To avoid a bloodbath, they surrendered and moved to the Cheyenne reservation in Oklahoma.

On the reservation, there was little food, and half the band died of malaria and pneumonia. Dull Knife and Little Wolf asked to be relocated to Montana, but U.S. agent John Miles suggested that they wait a year. Little Wolf replied that the Cheyenne would be dead in a year. A few weeks later, Miles angrily confronted Little Wolf when several Cheyenne ran away from the reservation, and he demanded hostages against their return. Little Wolf refused, and Miles threatened to withhold rations. Little Wolf replied, "Last night I saw children eating grass because they had no food. Will you take the grass from them?"

As a leader of the Northern Cheyenne, Little Wolf carried their Sacred Chief's Bundle, which meant that he was considered to be personally responsible for their welfare. So, Little Wolf and Dull Knife led their communities away from the reservation. Little Wolf planned the strategy that helped them evade the ten thousand U.S. soldiers who pursued them.

In Nebraska, he and Dull Knife separated. Several regiments of soldiers followed Little Wolf, but when his band saw soldiers, he

Little Wolf

always insisted that the Cheyenne should not be the first ones to shoot. Finally, one troop caught up with Little Wolf and persuaded him to surrender and come to Fort Keogh.

At Fort Keogh, the commanding general promised the Cheyenne a reservation in their home territory. Eventually, they were reunited with Dull Knife on a reservation in Montana's Rosebud Valley, having suffered far fewer casualties than Dull Knife's band.

Confinement on a reservation, even in the Cheyenne's home territory, was difficult. Little Wolf and several of his warriors enlisted in the U.S. Army as Indian scouts, a well-paying job that allowed them more freedom than they had on the reservation. Little Wolf lived for thirty more years, to about the age of eighty-four.

Red Cloud

Red Cloud was a leader of the Oglala Lakota, the largest group of the Sioux nation. He was the first Native American leader in the West to win a war against the United States, and he was also the last.

Red Cloud earned the respect of his community in his youth, as a warrior against the Pawnee, the Crow, the Ute, and the Shoshone. Until 1865, though, the Oglala remained at peace with settlers traveling through their territory. Then, gold was discovered in present-day Montana. The U.S. government tried to develop the Bozeman Trail for miners to travel on, building forts to protect the miners in the heart of Lakota hunting grounds. Red Cloud led the Great Plains nations to war, besieging one fort and cutting off its food supplies and effectively closing the wagon road.

In 1866, the U.S. government tried to negotiate for peace. The negotiations, held at Fort Laramie, looked promising until seven hundred troops arrived, expecting to erect a chain of forts along the Bozeman Trail. Furious, Red Cloud stormed out, accusing the peace commissioners of planning to take the country by force whether or not Native Americans signed the treaty.

Red Cloud began attacking troops traveling on the Bozeman Trail, and in one case, his warriors ambushed a regiment of soldiers, leaving no survivors. It became impossible to use the Bozeman Trail. When the government planned another peace conference in 1867, Red Cloud sent a message: "When we see the soldiers moving away and the forts abandoned, then I will come down and talk."

In 1868, the War Department finally evacuated the forts, which the Lakota and the Cheyenne burned to the ground. A few weeks later, Red Cloud signed a peace treaty. He had fought for several years to preserve his people's hunting grounds. Now, the soldiers were gone, the forts were destroyed, and the Bozeman Trail was closed. Red Cloud had won his war.

The treaty guaranteed the Lakota lands in the Dakota Territory, including the Black Hills and parts of Montana and present-day Wyoming. Red Cloud laid down his arms and settled on a Nebraska reservation.

The United States abided by its treaty for just a few years, until gold was discovered in the Black Hills. When the Lakota refused to sell the Black Hills, the United States went to war against them. Red Cloud had promised never to make war again, however, and during the war of 1876–1877, he kept his word.

In 1878, Red Cloud moved to the Pine Ridge Reservation, in present-day South Dakota. He spent his remaining years using peaceful methods to help his community, making several trips to Washington, D.C., to urge the U.S. government to keep the promises it made in its treaties.

Spotted Tail was a leader of the Brulé Sioux during the Plains Wars of the late 1800s. He advocated compromising with the U.S. government in order to prevent war, but he also worked hard to preserve traditional Sioux culture.

Like the Hunkpapa and Oglala Sioux, the Brulé lived in the western Great Plains. During Spotted Tail's first years as a warrior, the Sioux were constantly at war with the Pawnee, competing with them for access to hunting grounds. Spotted Tail showed his prowess in battles with the Pawnee, and he was chosen to be a war leader by the time he was thirty.

In 1855, U.S. troops attacked a Brulé village, after a cow belonging to a Mormon settler was killed by a Sioux. Spotted Tail led a retaliatory raid, killing all the men in the unit. More U.S. troops came, however, and in larger numbers. They killed eighty-six Brulés and captured seventy, including Spotted Tail's wife and baby daughter. To bring about peace, Spotted Tail and two other leaders went to Fort Laramie to give themselves up, expecting to be executed. Instead, they were imprisoned for about a year in Fort Leavenworth, Kansas. The Sioux respected Spotted Tail for his sacrifice and continued to consider him a war leader.

Spotted Tail allied himself with other Sioux groups that went to war after the massacre of Black Kettle's (see no. 21) community at Sand Creek in 1864. During Red Cloud's (see no. 29) war for the Bozeman Trail, however, he cooperated with U.S. officials, advising the Sioux not to fight. In 1868, Spotted Tail signed the Treaty of Fort Laramie, agreeing to a large South Dakota reservation for the Brulé. During the next several years, he frequently traveled with Red Cloud to Washington, D.C., to lobby on behalf of the Sioux.

When gold was discovered in the Black Hills, the United States offered the Sioux six million dollars for the land. Spotted Tail researched its value and asked for six hundred million dollars. The U.S. government refused. During the war that followed, Spotted Tail tried to negotiate a peace treaty. Eventually, he did negotiate the peaceful surrender of his nephew, Crazy Horse (see no. 41).

On the reservation, Spotted Tail worked to improve the lives of people in his community. He maintained a police force to keep liquor off the reservation, and he worked hard to prevent the U.S. Army from relocating the Sioux to present-day Oklahoma. When a Sioux warrior killed a settler, Spotted Tail turned him over to the government. Then, he used his own money to hire a lawyer for the man's defense. In the 1870s, some subchiefs plotted to overthrow Spotted Tail. In 1881, one of these subchiefs, Crow Dog, shot and killed him.

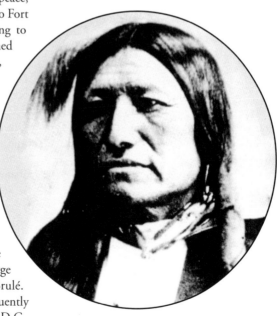

Spotted Tail

31. Victorio
(c. 1825–1880)

Victorio

Victorio, the successor to Mangas Coloradas (see no. 19) as leader of the Mimbreño Apache, had a desire to live in peace with Anglo settlers. Several times, he led his band to reservations, only to leave again when conditions proved to be intolerable. Victorio escaped the armies of the United States and Mexico so often that one army official called him the "greatest Indian general who had ever appeared on the American continent."

As a young man, Victorio fought alongside Mangas Coloradas against Mexico and the United States. When Mangas was killed, Victorio became the leader of the Mimbreño band, who were living at Ojo Caliente (Warm Springs). He fought Mexico and the United States for several years while also working to negotiate a peace.

In 1870, the Mimbreño agreed to live on what was supposed to be a permanent reservation, in their home territory in present-day New Mexico. In the spring of 1877, however, the U.S. government ordered Victorio's band to move to the San Carlos Reservation, in present-day Arizona. There, they would have to live with other Apache groups, some of whom were their enemies. Nonetheless, Victorio led his band to San Carlos, where they made an attempt to live in their new home.

By the fall of 1877, the Mimbreño were miserable in the hot, overcrowded reservation that one U.S. Army officer called "Hell's Forty Acres." Victorio left the reservation with three hundred Mimbreños. Using a combination of raids and diplomacy, he convinced officials to allow the Mimbreños to settle again at Ojo Caliente. The army agreed but then decided to relocate them to the Mescalero Reservation. At first, Victorio resisted this move, but then he agreed to it. In 1879, however, Victorio was indicted on an old charge of murder and horse-stealing. He fled the reservation with a group of Mimbreños and Mescaleros.

For more than a year, Victorio and his band lived as fugitives, moving back and forth between the United States and Mexico while being pursued by the armies of both countries. During this time, they somehow managed to remain in close contact with their friends and relatives on the Mescalero Reservation. Victorio's ability to avoid capture was especially remarkable because he and his warriors usually traveled with their families, including old people and children.

In 1880, the Mexican army trapped Victorio and his followers in the Tres Castillos Mountains. After two days of fighting, Victorio is said to have stabbed himself to death rather than accept captivity. Nearly eighty Mimbreños were killed in the battle, and the rest were captured.

38

Big Foot had the tragic honor of being the leader of a band of Sioux who were massacred by U.S. troops in 1890. The massacre took place at Wounded Knee Creek, South Dakota.

As a young man, Big Foot was regarded as a skillful negotiator. He often settled quarrels between rival groups, and he used diplomacy to avoid war whenever possible. He became the leader of the Miniconjou Sioux when his father died, in 1874. Big Foot allied himself with Sitting Bull (see no. 36) and Crazy Horse (see no. 41) during the Sioux War of 1876–1877, but he did not play a major role in the fighting.

After the war, Big Foot settled on the Cheyenne River Reservation and became one of the first Sioux to raise a corn crop there. He advised his community to retain its traditions while shifting to a farming economy. He also traveled to Washington, D.C., and lobbied for a school to be built on the reservation.

By 1890, conditions on the Plains reservations had reached their lowest point. The government had continued to take reservation land, and many Sioux were on the verge of starving because of the reduction of their hunting grounds. Corrupt agents often took money the U.S. government had earmarked for food and supplies for the reservations. In addition, U.S. government officials tried to wipe out the culture of the Native Americans by making their traditional clothing and religions illegal.

During this difficult time, many Sioux turned to a religion founded by Wovoka, a Paiute mystic. Wovoka preached that Native Americans could restore their old world by renouncing war and violence, praying to the Great Spirit, and performing a special dance and chanting. To do so would cause dead Native Americans to be resurrected, the buf-falo to return, and white settlers to leave. Many of Big Foot's followers embraced this religion, which whites called the "ghost dance" religion.

As the movement spread, the United States banned the religion and sent Lakota police to bring in Sitting Bull, who the U.S. government feared might lead a mass Indian uprising. Sitting Bull was killed during his arrest. Some Sioux leaders decided to bring their communities to the reservation headquarters for their own safety. Big Foot was considering such a move when troops arrived and arrested his band. The Miniconjou had heard how Sitting Bull had died, and they fled. U.S. soldiers captured them and escorted them to Wounded Knee Creek.

The soldiers began to disarm the Miniconjou. A gun went off somewhere, and the Seventh Cavalry began to fire. When the shooting stopped, more than two hundred Native Americans were dead, including Big Foot. Two-thirds of the Native Americans killed were women and children. The Battle of Wounded Knee Creek was the final battle of the Indian wars in the American West.

The dead body of Big Foot at Wounded Knee

Ely Samuel Parker
(1828–1895)

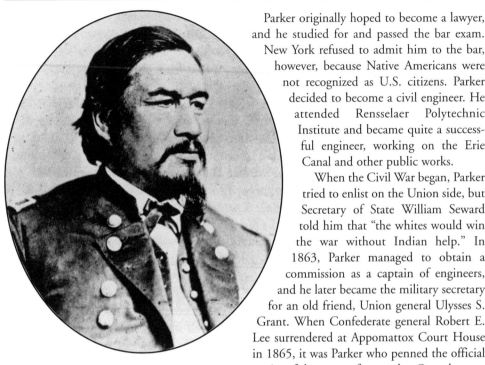

Ely Samuel Parker

Ely Samuel Parker, the first Native American to be Commissioner of Indian Affairs for the U.S. government, was born on the Tonawanda Reservation in New York State. He was the grandson of Handsome Lake (see no. 9), and he was the son of a Seneca chief.

Like many Native Americans of his generation, Parker began his education at a mission boarding school. Later, he attended private academies. As a teenager, he was such an able interpreter that he served as a translator for Seneca delegations to Washington, D.C. While still in his teens, Parker helped ethnologist Lewis Henry Morgan prepare a famous ethnography of the Iroquois. In his early twenties, Parker was honored with the title of "Keeper of the Western Door," an important office in the Iroquois Confederacy.

Parker originally hoped to become a lawyer, and he studied for and passed the bar exam. New York refused to admit him to the bar, however, because Native Americans were not recognized as U.S. citizens. Parker decided to become a civil engineer. He attended Rensselaer Polytechnic Institute and became quite a successful engineer, working on the Erie Canal and other public works.

When the Civil War began, Parker tried to enlist on the Union side, but Secretary of State William Seward told him that "the whites would win the war without Indian help." In 1863, Parker managed to obtain a commission as a captain of engineers, and he later became the military secretary for an old friend, Union general Ulysses S. Grant. When Confederate general Robert E. Lee surrendered at Appomattox Court House in 1865, it was Parker who penned the official copies of the terms of surrender. Over the next several years, Parker continued to serve in the army, working his way up to the rank of brigadier general.

After Grant was elected U.S. president, he appointed Parker the first Native American to be Commissioner of Indian Affairs. In that position, Parker worked to reform and restructure the Office of Indian Affairs, and he helped to generate public outrage over the U.S. Army's treatment of the Plains nations during the Plains wars.

Parker made many enemies as commissioner, and eventually, they accused him of defrauding the government. He was tried and found not guilty in the U.S. Congress. Parker resigned his position anyway, and he went on to make and lose a fortune in the stock market. He became the superintendent of buildings for the New York City Police Department and held that position until he died in 1895.

Standing Bear
(1829–1908)

Standing Bear

Standing Bear was a chief of the Ponca, a small nation related to the Omaha. After the U.S. Army forcibly moved the Ponca to present-day Oklahoma, he became famous for suing the army and winning his case.

A small nation of between eight hundred and nine hundred people, the Ponca worked hard to maintain peace with the United States. In 1858, they gave up all their land, except the area around the Niobrara River in present-day Nebraska, which was guaranteed by treaty as their permanent home. Then, in 1868, the United States accidentally awarded the Ponca's land to the Sioux, and the Sioux began trying to drive the Ponca off the land. In 1875, the U.S. government admitted it had made a mistake, and it proposed that the Ponca move to Oklahoma.

In 1877, agents of the Office of Indian Affairs escorted Standing Bear and several other Ponca leaders to Oklahoma, so they could pick a location for their new reservation. The Ponca leaders found all the suggested sites uninhabitable, and they refused to relocate. The agents told the leaders that if they wanted to return home, they would have to walk, so they did—for 500 miles (800 km).

When they arrived home, some Ponca had already been moved to Oklahoma. Standing Bear was jailed briefly for urging the Ponca to resist relocation. In May, about six hundred Ponca, including Standing Bear, were forced to march to Oklahoma at bayonet point. The journey lasted fifty days. Nine Ponca died on the way, including Standing Bear's daughter.

In Oklahoma, the Ponca suffered from starvation and malaria, and one third of them died during the first year, including Standing Bear's son. In the middle of winter, Standing Bear led sixty-six followers away from the reservation. They walked for two months, much of the time barefoot in the snow. Finally, they took shelter among the Omaha.

In the spring, U.S. general George Crook arrested Standing Bear and his followers, but he was shocked by their condition. When they related their story to him, Crook encouraged Thomas Henry Tibbles, a reporter, to publicize the story and file a lawsuit on behalf of Standing Bear.

In the case of *Standing Bear v. Crook*, Judge Elmer Dundy ruled that "An Indian is a person within the meaning of the law, and there is no law giving the army authority to forcibly remove Indians from their lands."

Standing Bear began to travel around the country, telling his story with Omaha interpreter Susette La Flesche (see no. 45). Eventually, he and his followers were allowed to live on their old Nebraska reservation, but most Ponca chose to remain in Oklahoma.

35. Geronimo
(c. 1829–1909)

Geronimo led one of the last bands of Apache to resist relocation to reservations. He fought so bravely, and evaded capture for so long, that his name became synonymous with a battle cry.

Born Goyathlay (One Who Yawns), he lived in an isolated community in the mountains, in what is now Arizona. His childhood was peaceful and undisturbed by any Anglo settlers. As a teenager, Geronimo joined Mangas Coloradas (see no. 19) and Cochise (see no. 26) in battles against Mexico. When he turned seventeen, Geronimo joined the council of warriors. In 1858, he went into Mexico. Upon returning home, he discovered that many of his friends and relatives, including his mother, his wife, and his three children, had been killed by Mexican soldiers.

For the next several years, Geronimo raided Mexico regularly, both for revenge and to get supplies for his community. According to some historians, he got the name Geronimo during these raids when terrified Mexican soldiers called on St. Jerome (in Spanish, *Jeronimo* or *Geronimo*) to help them. Other historians believe that the name Geronimo was a Spanish form of Goyathlay. During this period, Geronimo's courage earned him the respect of many warriors in his band.

In the 1870s, the U.S. Army forced thousands of Apache onto the San Carlos Reservation in present-day Arizona. For a few years, Geronimo and his followers lived in Mexico. Over the next decade, Geronimo was to come and go from the San Carlos Reservation several times. Much of the time, he and his followers lived in Mexico, raiding horses and cattle and killing settlers from the United States and Mexico.

The last time Geronimo left the reservation, in 1885, the U.S. Army pursued him. In March 1886, he surrendered in Mexico, only to flee with a small group as they approached the border. During this last campaign, Geronimo and sixteen warriors, twelve women, and six children were pursued by five thousand U.S. troops. They surrendered five months later, when the U.S. government promised, falsely, that after a short trip to Florida, they would be returned to Arizona. Geronimo and his followers were taken to Florida and then to Alabama, where one-fourth of them died of causes related to unsanitary living conditions.

Although some of his followers were allowed to return to the San Carlos Reservation, Geronimo was never to see his home again. The Comanche and the Kiowa, old enemies of the Apache, offered Geronimo part of their reservation at Fort Sill, Oklahoma. Geronimo accepted the offer, became a farmer, and converted to Christianity. In 1905, he published his memoirs. He died of pneumonia in 1909.

Geronimo

Warrior, chief, and holy man, the great Sioux leader Sitting Bull may well be the most famous Native American in history.

As a child, Sitting Bull was nicknamed "Slow," and he worked very hard to disprove the nickname. He became such a renowned warrior that his followers could intimidate their enemies just by shouting, "We are Sitting Bull's boys." In 1867, he became the principal chief of the Sioux, with Crazy Horse (see no. 41) as second-in-command.

In 1874, Colonel George Custer confirmed the presence of gold in the Black Hills in present-day South Dakota, an area the Sioux considered sacred. The U.S. government offered to buy the land for six million dollars, but the Sioux, relying on the research of Spotted Tail (see no. 30), asked for six hundred million dollars. The government refused and opened the land to miners.

In the middle of winter in 1876, the U.S. government sent a message that all Plains Native Americans not on reservations by January 31 would be considered hostile. The Sioux could not travel 240 miles (385 km), in bitter cold, in just a few weeks. Nevertheless, in March, U.S. troops set out to capture the Sioux.

On June 25, 1876, Custer led his Seventh Cavalry in an attack near the Little Bighorn River in present-day Montana. He did not realize that Sitting Bull had gathered there an alliance of several thousand Sioux and Cheyenne, including more than two thousand warriors. In the most famous battle in history between Native Americans and the U.S. military, Sitting Bull's warriors wiped out Custer's entire force of two hundred men.

The Sioux continued to win their battles, but they could not win the war. The buffalo, which they needed for food and supplies, was becoming extinct. Most Sioux eventually surrendered, but a few fled with Sitting Bull into

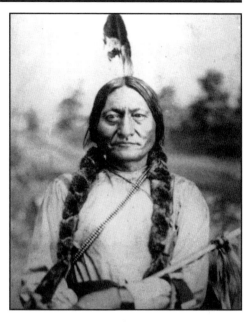

Sitting Bull

Canada. After four years, even they gave up. Sitting Bull moved to the Standing Rock Reservation, leaving briefly to tour with Buffalo Bill Cody's Wild West show. As the U.S. government took more reservation land, Sitting Bull, like Red Cloud (see no. 29), campaigned for the government to live up to its treaties.

In the late 1880s, many Sioux became "ghost dancers," practicing a new religion that claimed to be able to restore the Native American way of life. Although the ghost dance religion forbade violence, the U.S. government feared its followers would try to foment a rebellion, and it banned the religion. Sitting Bull supported the ghost dance movement, and in 1890, Office of Indian Affairs agents tried to arrest him. When his warriors tried to prevent the arrest, Sitting Bull was shot and killed. A few weeks later, the remaining ghost dancers were massacred with Big Foot (see no. 32) at Wounded Knee.

Kicking Bird

Kicking Bird was one of several Kiowa leaders. He led during a time when the Kiowa were deeply divided over whether to fight for their land or to make peace with white settlers. Kicking Bird favored peace, and he managed to convince most of his people not to go to war.

During Kicking Bird's youth, Little Mountain was the principal chief of the Kiowa. Kicking Bird became known as a valiant warrior, but he knew that Little Mountain felt their community's best hope was peace with the United States. In 1865, the Kiowa signed the Treaty of the Little Arkansas River, accepting a reservation in present-day Oklahoma.

Little Mountain died in 1866, leaving Kicking Bird as the leader of the peace faction of Kiowa and Satanta as the leader of the war faction. As a compromise, the community chose Lone Wolf, a militant leader who sometimes advocated peace, as their principal chief. The two factions, however, continued to struggle for control of the tribe.

In 1867, Lone Wolf and Kicking Bird both attended a peace conference with representatives of the U.S. government, along with representatives of the Cheyenne, Arapaho, Comanche, and Kiowa-Apache nations. Both leaders signed a treaty agreeing to a new, smaller reservation and the establishment of individual farm plots for families.

The following year, a group of Cheyenne were massacred at Sand Creek, making Kicking Bird even more determined to pursue a policy of peace. Members of the war faction began to call him a coward, so Kicking Bird led a raid into Texas, robbing a stagecoach and attacking an army unit.

The Texas raid was to be Kicking Bird's last act of violence. In the following years, he worked to promote peace. In 1873, he negotiated the release of Satanta and Big Tree, who had been arrested. This act earned him the loyalty of many people in his community. He prevented most Kiowa from joining their allies, the Comanche, in their war of 1873 to 1874.

Lone Wolf did go to war, however, and members of the war faction of the Kiowa constantly pressured Kicking Bird to consider doing the same. In 1874, the warring Kiowa were defeated, and Kicking Bird helped to negotiate their surrender. The U.S. Army asked Kicking Bird to identify the ringleaders to be imprisoned, and Kicking Bird named Lone Wolf and Mamanti.

Before he was taken to prison, Mamanti denounced Kicking Bird and threatened him. A few days later, Kicking Bird became ill while drinking a cup of coffee. Within a few hours, he was dead. An army doctor thought he had died of strychnine poisoning. Many Kiowa believed that Mamanti had caused Kicking Bird's death.

Datsolalee was one of the greatest weavers of the Washo, a nation renowned for its fine baskets. Today, her baskets are worth hundreds of thousands of dollars.

The Washo traditionally created fine baskets out of fern fibers and willow reed. The baskets, which incorporated complex geometric designs, were very difficult to make. The weaver used her teeth, fingers, a piece of sharp stone, and an awl to sew thirty-six stitches per inch. Datsolalee learned this skill at a young age and became very good at it. People said that she had "magic fingers."

When Datsolalee was still a teenager, the Washo lost a war with the Paiute, and the Paiute banned the Washo from basket weaving. The Paiute wanted to sell their own baskets without competition from the Washo weavers. The Washo economy was based on selling and trading baskets, and the next fifty years were a time of extreme poverty for the Washo people.

Despite the ban, Datsolalee and other Washo women did not stop weaving baskets. She was unable to sell her work, however, so she grew poor, along with the rest of the Washo. She married twice—her first husband died a few years after the marriage—and had several children.

In 1895, after her family had become severely poor, Datsolalee decided to defy the Paiute ban. She took some glass bottles she had covered with weaving to Carson City, Nevada, and she sold them to Abram and Amy Cohn, who owned a store there. From then on, the Cohns took charge of marketing Datsolalee's work for her.

Datsolalee's baskets were remarkably well-made, and they came to be prized by collectors everywhere. Her original, geometric designs were tiny and required exact spacing. Datsolalee made innovative changes to traditional designs, working with a new type of basket shape and adding a two-color design to her repertoire.

A very spiritual woman, Datsolalee apparently saw her designs first in visions and dreams. One of her most famous baskets, called "Myriads of Stars Shine Over the Graves of Our Ancestors," took her more than a year to complete. It contains 56,590 stitches, and it sold for $10,000 in 1930.

In her old age, Datsolalee lost much of her sight, but she continued to weave until she died, at the age of ninety. During her life, she produced nearly three hundred baskets, including forty extremely large pieces that came to be known as the "great treasures." Many of these large pieces are exhibited in museums around the world and, when sold in recent years, have cost as much as $250,000.

A Washo coiled willow basket

Lozen, the sister of Victorio (see no. 31), was unusual among Apache women because she chose never to marry and instead devoted herself to living as a warrior.

Many Apache women went to war, but they usually helped male warriors by setting up camp, cooking, and caring for the injured. Lozen did these jobs, but she was also a renowned fighter. Victorio described her as his "right hand," "strong as a man," and "braver than most." Respected as a Holy Woman, Lozen sat on decision-making councils. When the legendary Apache chief Geronimo (see no. 35) decided to surrender to U.S. authorities, he sent Lozen and Dahteste, another woman warrior, to arrange the surrender.

During Lozen's childhood, girls and boys alike were taught how to run, hunt, fight, follow tracks, and ride a horse. They also learned to cook and to sew. It was expected that, at times, their survival might depend on knowing how to perform all of these activities. So, as a child, Lozen learned horsemanship and how to use weapons. She often won foot races against boys her age.

During her puberty ceremony, Lozen, like other Apache girls, climbed into the mountains and fasted there for four days and four nights. While there, she was said to have been visited by spirits who gave her two powers: the ability to find the location of an enemy, and the ability to heal wounds. She was renowned for these abilities for the rest of her life.

Legend has it that Victorio's band relied on Lozen's powers to evade the U.S. and Mexican armies. She would look toward the sky, stretch out her arms, and turn in a circle while singing a prayer. Her hands would begin to tingle when she turned in the direction of a foreign army. When Victorio's band was defeated, Lozen was away helping a pregnant woman return to her family. Several warriors from the group believed that they would not have been cornered if Lozen had been with them.

After Victorio's death, Lozen joined Geronimo's band of Apache, among whom she soon developed a reputation for bravery. During one battle, she risked her life to recover a dropped bag of bullets, because the band was low on ammunition. Like the other warriors, however, Lozen knew that she could not survive as a fugitive forever.

At Geronimo's request, Lozen helped set up peace negotiations with the U.S. government. After the 1886 surrender, she was manacled and sent to Fort Marion, Florida, with Geronimo. The following year, the band was moved to Mobile, Alabama, where unsanitary living conditions resulted in the death of one out of every four of them. Lozen was among those who died.

Lozen (second row, third from right)

Chief Joseph, the younger Joseph of the Nez Percé, helped lead his people on what is considered the most brilliant retreat in the history of Native American-U.S. military warfare.

The Nez Percé, who lived in what is now Idaho, eastern Oregon, and Washington, had been at peace with the United States ever since Lewis and Clark first visited their lands in the early 1800s. They kept the peace even when settlers stole their horses and cattle. Joseph's father, Joseph the Elder, converted to Christianity, and young Joseph attended a mission school as a child.

According to an 1855 treaty, the Nez Percé were entitled to remain on a large reservation in their home territory. In 1863, however, gold was discovered in northeast Oregon, where Joseph lived. The U.S. government then convinced a few Nez Percé to sign a treaty reducing their territory by 6 million acres (2.4 million ha). They also agreed to move to an Idaho reservation. Joseph the Elder did not sign the treaty and, in a rage, tore his copy to pieces.

Joseph the Elder did not move his people to Idaho, and neither did his son, who became a leader of the Nez Percé after his father died. In 1877, General Oliver Howard threatened the Nez Percé and gave them a month to leave. To keep the peace, they prepared to go. Then, a few angry young warriors killed some white settlers. Expecting the entire community to be punished for the actions of a few, the Nez Percé decided to flee to Canada.

Some two hundred Nez Percé warriors and about five hundred women, elderly people, and children traveled more than 1,500 miles (2,400 km) through what is now Washington, Oregon, Idaho, and Montana, crossing the Rocky Mountains twice. Pursued by ten separate army commands, they defeated or fought to a standoff the two thousand soldiers who followed them, in thirteen battles and skirmishes. They used such skill that cadets at West Point still study their tactics today.

The Nez Percé leaders included several chiefs besides Joseph, and they would plan their strategy in war council meetings. It was Joseph, however, who became a symbol of the Nez Percé resistance. As he continued to elude capture and defeat, newspapers began to call him the "Indian Napoleon."

The Nez Percé War lasted through the summer and fall of 1877. The long trek ended when General Nelson Miles surprised the Nez Percé 30 miles (48 km) from the Canadian border. At first, they were taken to present-day Oklahoma, where many died of malaria. Joseph was eventually allowed to move to the Colville Reservation in Washington state. He made two trips to Washington, D.C., to speak on behalf of the Nez Percé before he died, in 1904.

Chief Joseph

As chief of the Lakota Sioux, Crazy Horse led his people to the most famous Native American victory over the U.S. Army in the history of the United States.

As a child, Crazy Horse was called Curly, because he had curly hair. At the time, the name Crazy Horse referred to his father. When Curly was about thirteen, he was living with his uncle, Spotted Tail (see no. 30). One day, Curly watched as a group of soldiers attacked Sioux leaders who were trying peacefully to mediate a dispute. Spotted Tail then led a group of warriors who killed the soldiers.

Some time later, Curly was away from the village, hunting buffalo. When he returned, the village was a burned wreck and eighty-six people lay dead. He rescued the one person he found alive, a Cheyenne woman. About 4 miles (6 km) away, Curly found more survivors. They told him that U.S. cavalry had attacked the village.

Curly returned to Lakota territory in 1857. That year, he performed many daring feats in a battle with the Crow. Curly's father gave Curly his own name, Crazy Horse, in recognition of Curly's deeds. His skills as a warrior were about to be tested.

In 1864, the Lakota learned of the Sand Creek massacre of Cheyenne led by Black Kettle (see no. 21). At the same time, the U.S. Army was beginning to build a road through Lakota territory to reach goldfields in present-day Montana. With Red Cloud (see no. 29) as their leader, the Lakota went to war and forced the army to abandon the project. After the war, Red Cloud agreed to live on a reservation, and Crazy Horse became the war chief of the Oglala, a band of the Lakota.

In 1876, Crazy Horse received a message from the U.S. government ordering the rest of the Sioux to move onto reservations. Instead, he joined Sitting Bull (see no. 36) and the ten thousand Sioux and Cheyenne camped with him on the Little Bighorn River. When Colonel George Custer attacked on June 25, Crazy Horse led the band that killed Custer and more than two hundred U.S. soldiers.

White Americans throughout the United States viewed this event as a massacre, and military reinforcements were quickly sent to pursue the Sioux, who continued to win other battles. Sitting Bull and Crazy Horse were running out of supplies, however, and the buffalo were dying. Sitting Bull left for Canada, but Crazy Horse led his followers to Red Cloud's reservation.

A few months later, Crazy Horse left the reservation without permission. On his way back, he was arrested. When he realized he was being led to jail, he began to struggle, and a soldier stabbed him with a bayonet. Crazy Horse died that night.

Crazy Horse

Activist Sarah Winnemucca is often considered the most famous Native American woman of the nineteenth century. For most of her life, she worked to obtain fair treatment for the Paiute.

When Winnemucca was born, the Paiute lived in a desert region that is now shared by Nevada, Oregon, and California. The Paiute had never met American settlers, because settlers usually journeyed around the desert. Winnemucca's grandfather, Chief Winnemucca, guided American explorer John Frémont to California, however, and as a child, Winnemucca sometimes traveled there with her grandfather. She learned to speak English and Spanish, as well as several Native American languages.

Winnemucca often interpreted for her father when he met with various people, such as U.S. Indian agents in charge of the reservations, U.S. army officers, and Native American leaders from other nations. She was confined to a reservation during the Paiute War of 1860 but worked for the army during later conflicts. She advocated for peace between the Paiute and the U.S. government, but violence continued to break out periodically. Some historians believe that Winnemucca's mother, sister, and brother were killed by U.S. soldiers.

Winnemucca frequently spoke out against abuses by U.S. Indian agents. Like many such agents, the Indian agents in charge of the Paiute reservation were corrupt. The agents stole food and supplies from the Paiute and did not

Sarah Winnemucca

stop white settlers from squatting on their lands. The Paiute grew poor, and in 1875, they were moved to Oregon's Malheur Reservation.

In 1878, some Paiute decided to join a related nation, Idaho's Bannock, in a war against the U.S. government. Winnemucca, however, became an interpreter and scout for the U.S. army. After the war, the government decided that all the Paiute involved in the war, regardless of which side they were on, should be relocated to Washington's Yakima Reservation.

They were forced to travel the 350 miles (560 km) to Yakima in the middle of winter. Lacking winter clothing, many Paiute died along the way, and others died shortly after their arrival because the housing and food on the reservation were so inadequate.

To call attention to the plight of the Paiute, Winnemucca delivered a series of lectures in San Francisco, California. She also wrote a book, *Life Among the Piutes*, which was the first published work written in English by a Native American woman.

U.S. president Rutherford B. Hayes agreed to meet with Winnemucca, and the U.S. secretary of the interior promised that the Paiute could return to Malheur. Funding for the move was not provided, however, and the Indian agent for Yakima refused to let the Paiute leave. The next year, the U.S. government opened Malheur to white settlers.

In Winnemucca's last years, she taught school and lectured along the East Coast. Winnemucca died of tuberculosis in 1891.

Quanah Parker led the Quahadi band of the Comanche in a war to save the buffalo. After the war, he became an important peacetime leader for the Comanche.

In 1836, the Comanche raided Fort Parker, a Texas settlement, and captured nine-year-old Cynthia Ann Parker. They raised her, and she grew to consider herself a Comanche. Eventually, she married a Comanche chief, Peta Nocona. With him, she had two sons, Pecos and Quanah, and a daughter, Topsannah.

In 1860, their lives were torn apart. Texas Rangers captured Cynthia Ann and Topsannah and fatally wounded Peta Nocona. The Rangers returned Cynthia Ann to the Parker family. In the next few years, she tried to escape several times. She is said to have died of a broken heart, after Topsannah died. Among the Comanche, Quanah's brother, Pecos, grew ill and died.

The next several years were difficult for Quanah as he mourned the loss of his family. He polished his hunting and war skills, however, and became a chief. It was also a difficult time for the Comanche nation. In 1867, the U.S. government called for the Comanche, Cheyenne, Kiowa, Kiowa-Apache, and Arapaho to settle on reservations in present-day Oklahoma. Most Comanche did, but the Quahadi branch, which Quanah belonged to, refused. They continued to live off the buffalo, and they periodically raided frontier towns for seven years. During this time, the Quahadi grew ever more desperate, as professional buffalo hunters gradually destroyed the buffalo herds.

In 1874, Quanah and other Comanche, Kiowa, Cheyenne, and Arapaho leaders led seven hundred warriors in an attack against twenty-eight buffalo hunters at Adobe Walls, beginning what came to be known as the Red River War. The buffalo hunters were armed with a cannon and with the newest technology—repeating rifles with a range of 600 yards (550 m). The warriors were forced to retreat. A few months later, the army captured or killed 1,500 horses belonging to the Indians and destroyed their tepees. In June 1875, Quanah and his band turned themselves in and relocated to Indian Territory in Oklahoma.

Quanah quickly adjusted to reservation life. He took up farming and ranching, began using his mother's last name, and learned to speak Spanish and English. He also became a peacetime leader of his community, negotiating leasing rights when cattle ranchers and investors wanted to use Comanche pastures.

He persuaded the Indian Agency to recognize him as the principal chief of the Comanche. As such, he frequently traveled to Washington, D.C., to represent Comanche interests, and he arranged to share the Comanche reservation with Apache leader Geronimo (see no. 35). When Quanah Parker died, in 1911, he was so beloved that the line of mourners following his funeral procession stretched for more than a mile.

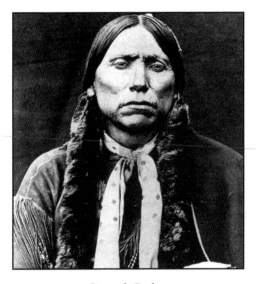

Quanah Parker

44. Plenty Coups
(c. 1848–1932)

Plenty Coups was the last chief of the Crow. He was their leader during their transition to reservation life.

When Plenty Coups was fourteen, he went into the mountains to do a vision quest. In his vision, he saw the buffalo disappear and cattle take their places. Then, there was a storm that only a chickadee survived. Plenty Coups and his community believed the dream meant that settlers would take over the Great Plains, and that, like the chickadee, the Crow could still survive.

Because of his vision, Plenty Coups urged his community never to go to war against the United States. He did wage war, however, against other Native American nations, especially the Lakota, who had killed two of his brothers and his parents. He was granted the name "Plenty Coups" after performing eighty heroic acts in battle.

Plenty Coups became a chief at about the age of twenty-five. During the Plains Wars, which were conflicts in the 1860s and 1870s between the United States and Plains nations such as the Sioux and the Cheyenne, he and other Crow warriors served as scouts for the U.S. Army. Crow warriors also assisted the army in its campaign against Chief Joseph (see no. 40) and the Nez Percé.

The Crow's early decision to cooperate with the U.S. government may have helped them avoid the tragic fate that befell some of their traditional enemies. The Crow were granted a reservation in their homeland in southern Montana. On the reservation, Plenty Coups, for the first time, stepped into the role of peacetime leader. He encouraged the Crow to take up farming and ranching but to keep practicing the traditional Crow religion.

Plenty Coups also continued to advocate Crow interests within the United States. When railroad companies wanted to lay tracks across Crow territory, for example, he insisted that the railroads hire Crow to work for them.

In his final years, Plenty Coups often negotiated with government representatives. He pressed for the Crow to receive a share of the profits when their land was leased to oil and gas companies. When the U.S. Congress tried to open the Crow reservation to settlers, Plenty Coups traveled to Washington, D.C., at least ten times to fight the plan, and he succeeded in blocking it.

In his will, Plenty Coups dedicated his farmland and home to be a memorial and museum for the Crow nation, to be "a reminder to Indians and white people alike that the two races should live and work together harmoniously." When Plenty Coups died in 1932, the Crow showed their respect for him by eliminating the title "chief," to make sure that Plenty Coups would be the last Crow leader ever to hold that honor.

Plenty Coups

45. Susette La Flesche
(1854–1903)

Susette La Flesche

Teacher, author, and lecturer, Susette La Flesche was an activist who worked tirelessly to advance the rights of Native Americans.

La Flesche grew up on the Omaha Reservation in present-day Nebraska. She attended the Presbyterian mission school on the reservation. Next, she traveled to New Jersey to attend the Elizabeth Institute for Young Ladies, becoming the first Omaha to seek her education outside her homeland.

After she graduated, La Flesche applied for a job teaching at a reservation school. At first, she did not get the job, but then she learned that reservation schools were required by law to hire qualified Native Americans if they applied. La Flesche wrote an angry letter to the Commissioner of Indian Affairs, and she was quickly hired.

In 1877, Standing Bear (see no. 34) led a group of Ponca from Indian Territory in present-day Oklahoma back to Nebraska. The Ponca and Omaha nations are closely related, so the Ponca took refuge among the Omaha. The U.S. army caught up with the Ponca and put them in jail, in preparation for sending them back to their reservation. The *Omaha Herald* publicized their plight, and several lawyers volunteered to help them sue the army.

At the trial, La Flesche testified on behalf of the Ponca, and she wrote several articles about the case. The court ruled that the Ponca could not be jailed without just cause, a decision that, for the first time, recognized Native Americans as having rights under U.S. law. After the trial, Susette, her brother Francis (see no. 53), and reporter Thomas Tibbles toured the country with Standing Bear.

On the lecture tour, Susette and Francis interpreted for Standing Bear. Susette also gave lectures, and she soon became a national celebrity known as "Bright Eyes." She advocated making Native Americans U.S. citizens, and she also called for the allotment of reservation lands to individual owners. La Flesche feared that the U.S. government could take land away from a nation much more easily than it could from individual citizens.

Thanks in part to her efforts, the U.S. government began a policy of land allotment. The policy did not seem to help, however, because swindlers often tricked new landowners into turning over the title to their lands. During this time, La Flesche also wrote a book with Standing Bear, *Ploughed Under: the Story of an Indian Chief.*

After the lecture tour ended, La Flesche and Tibbles got married. They continued to give lectures, raising awareness about living conditions on reservations. In 1886, they lectured in England and Scotland. A few years later, they reported together on the Wounded Knee massacre. They frequently lobbied the U.S. Congress on behalf of the Omaha and Ponca. La Flesche died in 1903.

Although his childhood education consisted of only a few years of mission school, Francis La Flesche became one of the first Native Americans to become a successful scholar and ethnologist.

Like his famous sisters, Susette (see no. 45) and Susan (see no. 51), Francis La Flesche grew up on the Omaha Reservation in present-day Nebraska. His father, Joseph La Flesche, the principal chief of the Omaha nation, made sure that Francis participated in traditional activities such as buffalo hunts and religious ceremonies. Joseph La Flesche had also converted to Presbyterianism, however, and he required his children to attend the reservation's Presbyterian mission school and learn English. He raised his children in a manner that allowed them to function within both the Native American and white cultures.

La Flesche and his sister Susette were fluent in English, so they were able to interpret for Ponca chief Standing Bear (see no. 34) when he toured the country giving lectures. On the tour, La Flesche met Alice Cunningham Fletcher, a famous ethnologist and Native American rights activist. He and Fletcher became close friends. After the tour, La Flesche went to work in Washington, D.C., as a clerk in the Office of Indian Affairs.

While he was working there, La Flesche spent his spare time researching Omaha culture with Fletcher. He traveled with her to Nebraska and interpreted for her among the Omaha. He persuaded several Omaha elders to explain the words and rituals for several religious ceremonies to both of them.

During the years of his association with Fletcher, La Flesche worked hard. In addition to his research on the Omaha, he returned to school, earning a bachelor's degree in law from National University in 1892 and a master's degree the following year. In 1893, he and Fletcher co-authored *A Study of Omaha Music,*

and in 1900, he published his own book, *The Middle Five*, a description of what it was like to attend a mission school on the Omaha Reservation.

In 1910, he transferred from the Office of Indian Affairs to the Smithsonian Institution's Bureau of American Ethnology. There, he could devote himself to ethnological research full time. In 1911, he and Fletcher published an exhaustive study of the Omaha, based on their research over the previous twenty years, called *The Omaha Tribe*.

La Flesche then began to study the Osage, a nation that was closely related to the Omaha. In his later years, after Fletcher's death in 1923, La Flesche published several important works on the Osage, including *Dictionary of the Osage Language*.

He received many professional honors for his scholarship. He was a member of the Washington Academy of Sciences and was granted an honorary doctorate from the University of Nebraska. La Flesche died on the Omaha Reservation in 1932.

Francis La Flesche

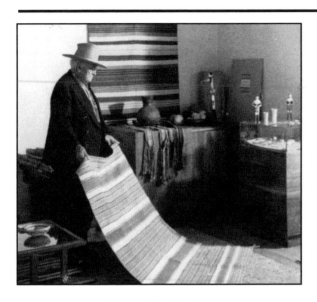

Henry Chee Dodge

Henry Chee Dodge was the last official head chief of the Navajo and their first tribal chairman. He was also a successful businessman and rancher.

Dodge's father died when Dodge was very young. When Dodge was about six, legendary frontiersman Kit Carson, who was a colonel in the New Mexico Volunteers Regiment, began destroying crops and livestock in order to force the Navajo to move to the Bosque Redondo Reservation in present-day New Mexico. Dodge's family fled.

One day, Dodge's mother left the camp to look for food and to ask her Hopi relatives to shelter the family. She never returned. Dodge was passed from family to family and finally, because of a mix-up, was accidentally left alone beside the trail. He met an eight-year-old girl and her grandfather, who adopted him. They took Dodge with them to Bosque Redondo, where they lived for four years until the Navajo were allowed to return home.

Dodge and his new family returned to the area around Fort Defiance, in New Mexico, where he was reunited with one of his aunts. There, he learned English and Spanish and attended the Fort Defiance Indian School. Then, he began working as a translator at his uncle's trading post. Eventually, he became the official Navajo interpreter for the U.S. Army.

In 1883, Dodge became the chief of the Navajo police, often interpreting during police investigations and mediating to prevent violent incidents. The following year, the government appointed Dodge as "head chief" of the Navajo, though he was not yet recognized as a leader by the Navajo communities.

Head chief was not a high-paying position, but since Dodge was unmarried, he had managed to save most of the salaries from his various jobs. By 1890, he could afford to invest in a trading post and sheep ranch. After his business was established, he married, and eventually, he had five children.

In the 1920s, Dodge and two other Navajo businessmen formed a council to handle requests for oil exploration leases on reservation land. From this council, the new Navajo Tribal Council was born, and in 1923, Dodge was elected as its first chairman. The council protected Navajo interests in negotiations with the U.S. government and with private corporations. In 1927, Dodge convinced the U.S. Congress that Navajos should receive 100 percent of the royalties from oil found under the reservation.

In 1928, Dodge resigned as council chairman to attend to his ranch. He was reelected to the council in 1942 and elected again in 1946, but he never took office after his last election. He contracted pneumonia and died the following year.

48. Charles Alexander Eastman (1858–1939)

Charles Alexander Eastman was one of the first Native Americans to earn a degree in medicine, but he was to become known as much for his writing as for his medical practice.

Eastman was left without his parents at an early age. His mother died giving birth to him, and when he was four, his father was sentenced to death for his role in the wars between the Sioux and the United States. Eastman fled with his grandmother and uncle into Canada. In his book *Indian Boyhood*, Eastman later described the thorough education he received among the Sioux in Manitoba, and the care his uncle took to help him become an astute observer of nature.

Throughout his childhood, Eastman expected that someday he would have to avenge his father's death. What Eastman didn't know was that his father had never been executed. U.S. president Abraham Lincoln had pardoned him, and he was serving time in an Iowa penitentiary. When Eastman's father was released from prison, he immediately searched for his fifteen-year-old son and brought him to live in the United States.

Eastman's father insisted that he enroll in a mission school. The contrast between Eastman's school days and his former life was extreme, but he was a good student and went on to attend Beloit College, Knox College, and Dartmouth University, where he earned a bachelor's degree in 1887. He then went straight to medical school at Boston University, earning his degree in 1890.

Right after graduation, Eastman became the doctor for the Pine Ridge Reservation in South Dakota. He was the only doctor to treat the victims of the massacre of Big Foot's band at Wounded Knee. The experience shocked him.

After three years working at Pine Ridge, Eastman opened a private medical practice. It was difficult to earn a living as a Native American doctor, however, because many settlers had racist attitudes toward Native Americans, and very few Sioux could afford to pay a doctor. In 1895, he went to work for the Young Men's Christian Association (YMCA), organizing thirty-two programs for Native American young people. Perhaps influenced by his wife, poet Elaine Goodale, Eastman also began to write.

Over the next twenty-seven years, Eastman wrote ten books and numerous articles on Native American culture and life. He also continued to practice medicine and to lobby on behalf of the Sioux in Washington, D.C. He worked on an Office of Indian Affairs project to give the Sioux legal names to protect their interests, and he served as a U.S. Indian inspector for reservations. He spent the last decade of his life lecturing in the United States and in England.

Charles Alexander Eastman

A painted pot by Nampeyo

Nampeyo, a Tewa potter, was perhaps the first Native American artist to become nationally and internationally famous for her work.

At a time when most women in her community had stopped adding decorative artwork to their pots, Nampeyo restored pottery-making to its status as an art form. Through her influence, Hopi women began to earn an income by making and selling pottery, improving the Hopi economy.

Nampeyo lived at Hano, a Tewa-Hopi community at First Mesa, one of the Three Mesas in northeastern Arizona where the Tewa and Hopi had lived for hundreds of years. There was no school in her area when Nampeyo was growing up. Like most children in her community at that time, she spent her days helping to carry water, grind corn, and plant crops.

She learned to make pots by watching her grandmother make pots for carrying water. She was fascinated by the process of collecting the clay, grinding it, and then shaping a pot by spiraling ropes of clay upward from the base. Nampeyo was lucky to have the chance to learn this art, because by this time, many Hopi women had begun to use metal pots and china bowls. Fewer and fewer of the Hopi women were making their own pots.

The Hopi lived in the same area their ancestors had, so Nampeyo could find very old fragments of pottery to study. In 1895, her husband helped archaeologists excavate an ancient Pueblo site. She studied the shards of pottery he found, sketching the designs she saw there. Later, she visited other archaeological sites to study more ancient pots.

Nampeyo began to decorate her own pots with designs inspired by the ancient potters. She used traditional methods to make the pots, prospecting for clay, pounding it with stones, removing impurities, and adding sand. She painted her pots using yucca brushes that she made herself, and she fired them in a traditional outdoor oven. The oven was so hot that she had to wet her hair first to withstand the temperatures.

Other women criticized Nampeyo's innovative pots. Wealthy tourists bought so many of them, however, that other potters began to copy her work. Nampeyo became famous, making trips to the Grand Canyon and to Chicago to demonstrate her pottery-making methods. In recent years, her work has been exhibited at the Smithsonian Institution and in museums around the world.

Late in her life, Nampeyo grew blind, probably through an eye infection caused by poor sanitary conditions. She kept making pots by touch, and her husband and daughters painted the pots for her. After she died, in 1942, seventy-three family members continued to make pots decorated in her style.

Charles Curtis was the first Native American elected to the U.S. Senate, and the first to become vice president of the United States.

Curtis was only one-eighth Kaw, but his mother made sure he was listed on the tribal rolls and planned for him to live on the reservation. She did not want Curtis to be excluded from any Kaw land settlements. When Curtis was three years old, however, his mother died. From then on, his paternal grandparents and his maternal, Kaw grandparents, Louis and Julie Pappan, shared custody of him.

Curtis spoke Kaw and fit comfortably into reservation life. He also enjoyed living in Topeka, where his paternal grandfather owned a race track. At the age of nine, Curtis rode in his first race, and he soon became a famous jockey, known throughout Kansas as "the Indian Boy."

In 1873, Curtis left Topeka to meet the Pappans, who were traveling with the rest of the Kaw to Indian Territory in present-day Oklahoma. Curtis wanted to live with the Pappans, but both of his grandmothers wanted him to finish school in Kansas, which he did. Afterward, he went to law school.

Curtis entered politics in 1884. He ran for office and became the Shawnee county attorney. In 1892, he was elected to the U.S. House of Representatives, where he served on the Territories Committee and the Committee on Indian Affairs.

During Curtis's lifetime, some Native Americans fought to maintain the sovereignty of their nations. Other Native Americans, including Curtis, believed that individual Native Americans would be better off if they assimilated into the mainstream of American culture. Curtis advocated a policy of allotment, which involved dissolving tribal governments and parceling out tribal land to individual members of each Native American nation.

In 1898, he drafted the "Curtis Act," which abolished tribal courts, prevented tribal laws from being enforced in federal courts, and specifically allotted the lands and dissolved the governments of the Cherokee, Choctaw, Chickasaw, Creek, and Seminole nations. (In recent times, both tribal courts and tribal governments have been restored.)

Curtis was elected to the U.S. Senate in 1907. He served there for twenty years. In 1923, he was elected Senate Majority Leader.

In the 1928 U.S. presidential race, Curtis was a candidate for the Republican nomination against Herbert Hoover. Curtis ran a quiet campaign, hoping to emerge as a compromise candidate. When Hoover won the nomination, party loyalists wanted someone from a farm state to balance the ticket, and Curtis and Hoover were stuck with each other. They won the election, but Curtis never played an important role as Hoover's vice president.

After he and Hoover lost the 1932 election to the Democratic ticket, headed by Franklin D. Roosevelt, Curtis retired from politics.

Charles Curtis

Susan La Flesche

Susan La Flesche was the first Native American woman to become a doctor trained in Western medicine. As the reservation physician for the Omaha, she also frequently represented them in negotiations with the U.S. government.

La Flesche was raised on the Omaha Reservation and attended a mission school there. As a teenager, she followed in the footsteps of her sister Susette (see no. 45), traveling to New Jersey to attend the Elizabeth Institute for Young Ladies. In 1884, Susan enrolled at the Hampton Institute, a school that was originally founded to educate freed African American slaves.

After graduation, she obtained a scholarship to the Woman's Medical College of Philadelphia. Her decision to become a doctor was notable not only because there were very few Native American or women physicians at the time, but also because the Omaha tradition was for men, not women, to become healers.

La Flesche graduated at the top of her class and soon became the reservation physician for the Omaha. At the time, it was very rare for Native Americans to be appointed to such a post, and La Flesche was the first Native American woman to hold such a position.

As the only doctor for 1,300 people, La Flesche worked from dawn until well after dark each day, driving her horse and buggy over miles of country roads to reach her patients. She managed to contain several epidemics of smallpox, influenza, and diphtheria, but she also worked so hard that she damaged her own health. In 1893, La Flesche resigned her post to recover and to care for her sick mother.

In 1894, La Flesche married Henry Picotte, despite her parents' objection that Picotte was known to be a heavy drinker. She opened a private practice in Bancroft, Nebraska, and continued to work hard, caring for her patients, raising two sons, and giving lectures about health-related issues.

Her husband died in 1905 of an alcohol-related illness, and she became a Presbyterian missionary to the Omaha. She also became an informal representative for the Omaha in negotiations with the government. In one case, she traveled to Washington, D.C., even though she was terribly ill, after Omaha officials begged her to do so. In Washington, she met with the secretary of the interior and convinced him that Omaha landowners should be able to control their own property, rather than having it held in trust on their behalf.

La Flesche's final accomplishment was the opening of a hospital in Walthill, Nebraska. She had campaigned for years to get the hospital built. She died there in 1915, after a long illness.

52. Amos Bad Heart Bull
(1869–1913)

Amos Bad Heart Bull belonged to the Oglala Lakota, one of the Sioux nations. He is known as the Herodotus of his people. Like Herodotus, a historian of ancient Greece, Bad Heart Bull documented decades of his people's history. His chronicles included illustrations and captions.

Bad Heart Bull's father was the Oglala's official historian, recording important events from each year on buffalo hide. He died young, however, and Bad Heart Bull was raised by his uncles. They told him stories about important battles in which they had fought. As a child, Bad Heart Bull loved to listen to these stories, and he collected copies of treaties and other documents relating to negotiations between the Lakota and the United States. He never went to school, but he taught himself how to draw. He also taught himself to read and write, using symbols that missionaries used to transcribe Lakota words. In 1890, Bad Heart Bull enlisted in the U.S. Army as a scout, and he learned English.

At some point, Bad Heart Bull obtained a used ledger. At the time, paper was a precious commodity, and Native American artists frequently painted and drew in used ledger books. The practice was so common that, for a time, all Native American art on paper was called "ledger art."

Bad Heart Bull used his ledger book to begin a series of 415 drawings. For the next twenty years, he worked at recording the history of the Oglala. He gathered information from people who had lived through historical events, listening to their stories. Then, he created illustrations depicting the events and wrote captions explaining what was happening in each picture. He also drew the only known picture of his cousin, Crazy Horse (see no. 41).

Bad Heart Bull's technical skill as an artist was extraordinary. He first drew a panoramic long-shot view of an event. Then, he added framed close-ups, set off to one side, so that the viewer could see the effects of the event on individual people who were there. His pictures form an invaluable record for historians today, for two reasons. He captured small details of everyday Oglala life, and he presented events very objectively, bringing the accounts of many people into a unified whole.

Little is known about Bad Heart Bull's life apart from his work. He died in 1913, and his ledger book passed to his sister, Dolly Pretty Cloud. In 1926, University of Nebraska graduate student Helen Blish persuaded Pretty Cloud to let her study and photograph it. The photographs were published as the book *A Pictographic History of the Oglala Sioux*. The original was buried with Pretty Cloud when she died, in 1947.

An illustration of the Battle of Little Bighorn, by Amos Bad Heart Bull

Gertrude Simmons Bonnin

Writer and activist Gertrude Simmons Bonnin helped to bring about important reforms in the U.S. government's policy toward Native Americans.

Gertrude Simmons was born on the Yankton Sioux Reservation in present-day South Dakota, in the same year as the Battle of the Little Bighorn. She grew up at a time when U.S. Indian agents and missionaries were pushing Native Americans to give up their culture. Simmons and her mother resisted this process.

Against her mother's wishes, however, Simmons enrolled in a boarding school run by Quaker missionaries. She did not speak English, and teachers beat students if they spoke Sioux, so Simmons had a difficult time there. She learned English, and she remained at the school for several years.

Simmons then enrolled at Earlham College and studied to be a teacher. She taught briefly at Carlisle, a school for Native Americans in Pennsylvania. She left the school, though, because its founder believed that Native Americans should be trained as farmers or laborers and not educated in academic subjects.

Simmons moved to Boston, and while there, she began submitting short stories and essays to magazines, using the pseudonym Zitkala-Sa, or Red Bird. She was published in several national periodicals, including *Harper's* and the *Atlantic Monthly*. In her writings, Simmons criticized the educational practices of white reformers.

In 1902, Simmons married Richard Bonnin, who, like Simmons, was a Nakota, or Yankton, Sioux. They moved to Utah, where they both worked for the Office of Indian Affairs. Disturbed by the poverty she saw on reservations, Bonnin began working with the Society of American Indians (SAI). She became SAI's secretary and moved to Washington, D.C., so that she could lobby the U.S. Congress on SAI's behalf.

Bonnin resigned from SAI in 1920, but she continued to work as an activist. During the 1920s, she persuaded a women's club to form the Indian Welfare Committee. This committee studied reservation living conditions, which, in many cases, were severely poor, and it pressured the U.S. government to conduct a follow-up investigation. As a result, Congress hired a research firm, which verified many of the Indian Welfare Committee's findings. The firm's report, called the Meriam Report, led to important reforms in government policy.

At the same time, Bonnin was working with the Indian Rights Association to study the theft of land from Native Americans in Oklahoma. In 1924, she co-wrote an exposé showing that swindlers had tricked many Native Americans into giving up land on which oil had been discovered.

During Bonnin's lifetime, Congress did pass some of the legal reforms that she had worked so hard to bring about. In 1924, Native Americans were granted U.S. citizenship. In 1934, Congress allocated money to pay for health care and schools on reservations.

Cherokee humorist Will Rogers was one of the most beloved entertainers of the early twentieth century.

Rogers grew up on his family's ranch in present-day Oklahoma. He went to his first cattle roundup as a toddler and learned to throw a rope before he was five years old. Rogers loved to do rope tricks and won his first prize for roping at the age of twenty. So, it's no surprise that he began his career as an entertainer doing rope tricks in wild west shows.

As a young man, he had been working as a cowhand and managing his father's ranch, but in 1901, he left for Argentina. He traveled the world, tending cattle and working in wild west shows and circuses in South Africa, New Zealand, and Australia. Then, he returned to the United States and became a "rope artist and rough rider" in various wild west shows.

One day, Rogers began telling jokes about current events as he did his tricks. Rogers loved reading newspapers, and he found enough material there to provide jokes for three daily performances. He didn't confine himself, however, to joking about current events. Rogers was proud of his Cherokee ancestry, and he sometimes remarked, "my ancestors didn't come over on the Mayflower, but they met the boat."

Audiences loved Rogers's down-to-earth, nonpartisan approach to entertainment. By 1912, he had begun appearing on stage and then later in movies, and he was a big success in both. In 1922, he started writing a humorous column on the news for the *New York Times*. For a while, he was the most widely read newspaper columnist of his day. In 1930, he began a weekly radio show.

Many people admired Rogers for his efforts to help charitable causes. He gave the Red Cross one hundred dollars a week for the duration of World War I. During the Depression, he donated a percentage of his earnings from each radio broadcast to the Red Cross and the Salvation Army. At various times, he gave performances to benefit flood victims, earthquake victims, farmers, and the unemployed.

Rogers was one of the country's earliest flying enthusiasts. He flew to most of his engagements around the country, at a time when few U.S. planes carried passengers, and most people considered flying to be dangerous. If he could not catch a passenger flight, he would ride a mail plane, weighing himself and paying his fare as if he were a package being shipped.

Unfortunately, Rogers's love of air travel led to his death. He was killed in a plane crash, along with aviation pioneer and pilot Wiley Post, near Barrow, Alaska. Rogers's epitaph reads, "I never met a man I didn't like."

Will Rogers

Maria Martinez

Maria Martinez is probably the most famous Native American potter of the twentieth century. Like Nampeyo (see no. 49), she revitalized the Pueblo economy in her community and transformed pottery-making from a craft into an art.

Martinez was born in San Ildefonso Pueblo, a Tewa farming town in present-day New Mexico. When she was about seven years old, her aunt taught her to make pottery. Like Nampeyo, Martinez was fortunate to have the chance to learn this skill, because many Pueblo were beginning to use metal pots instead of clay ones. By the time Maria was thirteen, she was a skillful potter.

As a young woman, Maria married an old friend, Julian Martinez. For the rest of his life, Julian collaborated with Maria to make pottery. In 1907, he helped some Smithsonian Institution archaeologists excavate an ancient Pueblo ruin. One of the archaeologists asked Maria to try to duplicate the ancient Pueblo pots, using broken shards as a guide. The shards were thinner than the pots Maria usually made. Experimenting, she discovered that she could make equally thin pots if she mixed the clay with a very fine sand.

From 1909 to 1912, Maria and Julian demonstrated pottery-making at the Museum of New Mexico. Maria shaped the pots, and Julian painted them. They studied the museum's artifacts, trying to duplicate the black ones, and discovered that they could blacken pots with smoke.

By 1919, Julian had begun to paint the pots with white paint before they were fired, creating designs that also appeared in black but with a matte texture. These were the pots that were to make Martinez famous, but at first, she hid them under the bed, embarrassed that they did not look like the multicolored pots people in her community had been creating for years.

Traditionally, Pueblo potters did not sign their work, because they did not approve of calling attention to individual accomplishments. Martinez's customers begged her to sign her pots, however, so that they could prove the pots were authentic, and in the 1920s, she became the first Pueblo potter ever to sign her pots. In keeping with the Pueblo emphasis on the good of the community, she often gave her profits to those in need, and she also taught other potters to make the black-on-black pots.

In 1943, Julian Martinez died, and Maria Martinez's daughter-in-law, Santana, began painting her pots for her. Then, in 1956, Martinez began to collaborate with her grandson, Popovi Da. She continued to teach and collaborate with others until her death in 1980.

Martinez received many national and international awards for her work, including several honorary doctoral degrees. Today, her pots sell for as much as twenty thousand dollars.

Clinton Rickard
(1882–1971)

Clinton Rickard helped found the Indian Defense League of America (IDLA), and he fought hard to preserve the sovereignty of Native American nations.

Rickard grew up on a farm in the Tuscarora Reservation in western New York. When Rickard was a young boy, his alcoholic father abused him, as well as Rickard's brothers and mother. Once, Rickard and his brothers hid in the outhouse from their father, who was trying to shoot them. Afterward, Rickard vowed never to drink alcohol. He later said he prayed that one day he would be able to protect others from harm.

He attended school occasionally but spent most of his time working on the farm and in a local lumber mill. He only completed a third-grade education. When the Spanish-American War began in 1898, Rickard joined the U.S. Army, partially to escape his father. The only Native American in his brigade, he served honorably, once saving his captain's life. After the war, he returned home, to farm and raise a family. Rickard was married three times—his first two wives died prematurely—and he had thirteen children.

During the 1920s, Rickard became a chief of the Tuscarora and a member of their governing council. He also gained an interest in civil rights. Unlike such as activists as Gertrude Simmons Bonnin (see no. 53), Rickard was strongly opposed to making Native Americans U.S. citizens. He stated, "We had our own citizenship. ... How can a citizen have a treaty with his own government?" He believed that the United States might be less likely to keep its treaties with Native American nations if Native Americans were U.S. citizens. (When Rickard joined the army, he felt he was following a Tuscarora tradition of fighting as allies alongside the United States.)

In 1926, Rickard helped establish the IDLA, which was originally the Six Nations Defense League. This organization provides lawyers to Native Americans who cannot afford them. It also lobbies the U.S. Congress and the Canadian government to respect the civil rights of Native Americans. IDLA achieved its first victory in 1928, when Canada and the United States agreed to respect the rights of Native Americans to freely cross the U.S.-Canadian border to visit relatives and to trade.

For the next forty-five years, Rickard worked with IDLA to preserve the sovereignty of Native American nations. He managed to obtain congressional recognition of parts of the Jay Treaty of 1794 and the 1814 Treaty of Ghent. He also worked to protect the civil liberties of Native Americans, to free from jail Native Americans who were falsely accused of crimes, and to open high schools in the state of New York to Native American students.

Clinton Rickard

Charles Albert Bender was one of the greatest baseball pitchers of the twentieth century. He was the first Native American to be inducted into the Baseball Hall of Fame.

A member of the Ojibwa, Bender was born and raised in Brainerd, Minnesota. He was one of thirteen children. Bender spent his early childhood on the White Earth Chippewa Indian Reservation, but, like many Native American children of his generation, he was sent to boarding school. He attended Pennsylvania's Carlisle Indian School, and while there, he played on the baseball, football, basketball, and track teams. In college, he played baseball and football.

In 1902, a scout for professional baseball's Philadelphia Athletics discovered him while he was pitching for the Harrisburg Athletic Club, a semiprofessional organization. Athletics manager Connie Mack, who was also part owner of the franchise, quickly offered him a contract. Bender played for the A's for the next twelve years.

Pitching for the A's, Bender became a sports legend. He created a special pitch, still used by pitchers today, called a slider, or "nickel curve." It has been described as halfway between a fastball and a curveball. Mack quickly learned that Bender was the pitcher he needed for "must win" games. Ty Cobb called him "the smartest pitcher I ever faced."

Bender helped lead the A's to five World Series appearances and three world championships. His best year was 1910, when his winning percentage was .821, with a 23-5 record and a 1.58 ERA. In a career that spanned fifteen years, Bender won 210 games and lost only 127, for a winning percentage of .623. He also won another six games in his five World Series appearances.

As one of the first Native Americans to play major league baseball, Bender endured racial taunts and stereotyping on a regular basis. The fans nicknamed him "Chief" Bender, although he was not an Ojibwa chief. He didn't care for the nickname and always signed his autographs with his own name. When people jeered at him, doing "war whoops," Bender would shout back, "foreigners!"

In 1914, the Baltimore Terrapins, a team in the new Federal League, offered Bender and some other A's players more money if they would "jump" from the established major leagues. Bender agreed, and his last season was marred by Mack's suspicions that he was about to leave the team. After one season with the Terrapins, Bender returned to the majors in 1916, and he played for the Philadelphia Phillies for two seasons. After he retired, he coached for several teams, including the A's.

Bender was elected to the Baseball Hall of Fame in 1953. He died of cancer the following year.

Charles Albert Bender

Clarence Tinker became the highest ranking Native American officer in United States military history. A World War I hero, he commanded the U.S. Air Force in Hawaii during World War II, until he was shot down in the Battle of Midway.

Tinker was only one-eighth Osage. He was the son of a part-Osage man, George Ed Tinker, and a non-Osage woman, Rose Jacobs Tinker. He was raised as a member of the Osage nation in present-day Oklahoma.

As a young man, Tinker worked on his father's news-paper, the *Wah-Sha-She News*. He attended an Osage boarding school as a child, and he later attended another school for Native Americans, the Haskell Institute, in Lawrence, Kansas. The school that probably had the greatest influence on his later career, though, was the Wentworth Military Academy, in Lexington, Missouri.

U.S. planes attack at the Battle of Midway

In 1908, Tinker was commissioned as a second lieutenant in the Philippine police force. At the time, the Philippines were being governed by the United States. Officers in the police force, the Philippine Constabulary, were originally drawn from the U.S. military. Tinker served in the Philippines for five years. Then, he became a lieutenant in the U.S. Army, serving in Hawaii. After serving in World War I, he became interested in the new, and rapidly developing, technology of flying.

Tinker entered the Air Service and became a pilot. In 1927, he was named commandant of the Air Corps Advanced Flying School. During the 1930s, he commanded several pursuit and bombardment units and air bases. At one point, on duty in London, he received the Soldier's Medal for rescuing a pilot from a crash scene. In 1940, Tinker became a brigadier general. In December 1941, Japan bombed U.S. forces at Pearl Harbor, and Tinker was placed in charge of reorganizing Hawaii's air defenses.

Native Americans were enlisting in the U.S. armed forces in great numbers. During World War II, 44,000 Native Americans served, fighting on all fronts. According to army historians, no other group made a greater per capita contribution to the war effort.

Many Native Americans became war heroes, including Tinker. In 1942, he was promoted to major general. The same year, he chose to lead a bomber squadron against the retreating Japanese navy during the Battle of Midway. His plane was fired upon and plunged into the ocean. Tinker and the eight others on board were killed. Tinker's body was never found. He was survived by his wife, daughter, and two sons. A few months later, Tinker Air Force Base, in Oklahoma City, Oklahoma, was named in his honor.

Jim Thorpe

Jim Thorpe is considered by many people to be the best all-around athlete of the first half of the twentieth century. He excelled at every sport he ever tried, and he made sports history at the 1912 Stockholm Olympics.

A member of the Sauk-Fox nation, Thorpe was the great-grandson of Black Hawk (see no. 14). He grew up in present-day Oklahoma, where Black Hawk's descendants were moved after they were ousted from their land in Illinois and Iowa.

As a child, Thorpe attended first a mission school and then Haskell Institute, in Lawrence, Kansas. Then he enrolled at Carlisle Industrial Indian School, a famous vocational school for Native Americans in Pennsylvania. It was at Carlisle that Thorpe began his athletic career.

While there, he lettered in ten sports: football, baseball, track, boxing, wrestling, lacrosse, gymnastics, swimming, hockey, and basketball. He also won prizes for his marksmanship, and in his spare time, he played golf. In 1911 and 1912, Thorpe was an all-American football player, and he helped Carlisle defeat some of the best college football teams of those years, such as Harvard, Army, and Pennsylvania.

In the summer of 1912, Thorpe headed to Stockholm, Sweden, with the U.S. Olympic team. His performance at the Olympics was historic. He won both the pentathlon and the decathlon, winning the decathlon with a score almost seven hundred points ahead of the second-place finisher. It was to be thirty-six years before another Olympic athlete performed as well in the decathlon.

Unfortunately, a few months later, the Olympic Committee took Thorpe's medals back, because he had played professional minor league baseball during summers off from Carlisle. The decision was always controversial, with many people feeling that Thorpe had been penalized unfairly for a minor rules infraction. In 1982, the International Olympic Committee restored his records and medals.

Returning home, Thorpe became a professional football and baseball player, helping to make football a popular American sport. He played for the Canton Bulldogs, the team that won the title of "world champion" in 1916, 1917, and 1919. In 1920, Thorpe became the first president of the American Professional Football Association. Two years later, it became the National Football League. He also founded and played on an all-Native American team, the Oorang Indians.

After retiring from sports, Thorpe worked at various jobs, including managing recreation for the Chicago Park System, lecturing on sports and Native American issues, and sailing with the Merchant Marine.

In 1950, sportswriters and broadcasters for the Associated Press named Thorpe "the greatest American football player" and the "greatest overall male athlete" for the first half of the twentieth century. Three years later, he died of a heart attack.

A linguist, ethnologist, and novelist, Ella Cara Deloria was determined to make sure that Sioux language and culture did not disappear, as they had for so many other Native American nations.

Deloria was the daughter of Philip Deloria, one of the first Sioux to become an Episcopal priest. Her parents raised her as both a Sioux and a Christian. As a child, she attended the Standing Rock Reservation mission school and the All Saints School, in Sioux Falls, South Dakota. A good student, she won a scholarship to Oberlin College. After two years at Oberlin, she transferred to Columbia University.

At Columbia, Deloria assisted Franz Boas, a scholar who is known as the "Father of Modern Anthropology." Boas paid Deloria eighteen dollars a month to translate Lakota Sioux texts. After Deloria graduated, in 1915, she returned home to care for her sick mother and aging father. After her mother died, her sister, Susan, developed benign brain tumors that caused her to have major health problems. Deloria took care of Susan for the rest of Susan's life, a situation that made it even more difficult for her to pursue her scholarship.

In 1927, Deloria began working for Boas again, translating Sioux texts and doing fieldwork. She interviewed Sioux elders, recording Sioux stories, history, and customs. Deloria had never studied anthropology and did not consider herself an anthropologist. She did, however, feel a personal mission to document Sioux culture.

It was not an easy way to make a living. Deloria was always short of money, and she had to sell some of her family's land to pay her expenses. For a while, she and her sister Susan had to live out of her car while she conducted her fieldwork.

After several years, Deloria published *Dakota Texts*, a book of traditional Sioux stories. Nine years later, she co-authored *Dakota Grammar* with Franz Boas. Both books are still used by linguists and anthropologists today. She also wrote a book about Sioux culture, *Speaking of Indians*. Deloria managed to collect the largest body of information ever compiled about any Plains nation.

She also wrote a novel, *Waterlily*. The story of the life of a Sioux woman, the book explained details of Sioux women's lives that male anthropologists at the time never bothered to study. Publishers refused to publish it, because they believed that no one would want to read about a Native American woman.

Deloria continued to research Sioux culture until she died of pneumonia, in 1971. At the time of her death, she was working on a Sioux dictionary. The University of Nebraska Press finally published *Waterlily* in 1988. Largely because of Deloria's work, Sioux language and culture are better documented than those of almost any other Native American nation.

Ella Cara Deloria

Lucy Lewis

Lucy Lewis is one of the Southwest's most famous potters. As a child, she made ashtrays that sold for a few cents each. Much later in life, she began making carefully crafted pots that became recognized nationally and internationally as important works of art.

Lewis grew up on a mesa at Acoma Pueblo, in present-day New Mexico. When she was seven or eight years old, her aunt taught her to make pottery. She made pots to sell to tourists and then rode on horseback with her mother to a train station, 17 miles (27 km) away. At the station, she could sell the pots for five or ten cents each.

She married during her teen years, and she continued to make pots for tourists to supplement her family income. As the years pro-gressed, she had very little spare time. Her days were filled with planting gardens, raising livestock, and caring for her nine children. When she had time for pottery-making, she worked as fast as she could to maximize her profits, sometimes painting more than one hundred pots a day.

Later, Lewis began to craft her pots much more carefully. She still made pots to sell to tourists, decorated with popular bird and flower designs. Sometimes, however, she painted designs of her own, inspired by shards of ancient pots that she found in the dust on the mesa. She developed fine-line designs in which an outline was filled in with parallel lines.

It was against Pueblo custom for an individual to call attention to herself or her own work. In 1950, Lewis broke with this tradition by exhibiting a fine-line pot in the Gallup Intertribal Ceremonial in Gallup, New Mexico. Lewis's pot won a blue ribbon, and art lovers began to collect her creations. Lewis had always signed her pots simply "Acoma Pueblo," but now she began to sign her own name as well.

Although Lewis's fame went against Pueblo tradition, she used only traditional methods to make her pots. She prospected the clay, ground it, and mixed sand into it. Unlike Nampeyo (see no. 49) and Maria Martinez (see no. 55), Lewis did not study pots found at archaeological sites or displayed in museums. Her creations were based simply on ancient shards she found and on her own imagination.

Lewis was known for several innovations in pottery-making: her fine-line technique, her use of the Zuni heart-line deer, and her use of empty space. She added dramatic effects, such as a small black figure or black geometric shapes placed asymmetrically, to a white background. Lewis continued to make pottery until she died, in 1992.

62. Ben Reifel
(1906–1990)

Ben Reifel is best remembered for being the first member of the Sioux nation to be elected to the U.S. House of Representatives. He dedicated much of his adult life to public service and improving the lives of Native Americans.

The son of a Brulé Sioux mother and a German-American father, Reifel was born on South Dakota's Rosebud Reservation. Reifel's mother encouraged him to pursue an education, but his father wanted him to stay at home and work on the farm. As a result, Reifel did not finish the eighth grade until he was sixteen. His father would not allow him to go to high school, but Reifel was determined, so he ran away and enrolled in a high school 250 miles (400 km) from home. After graduation, he attended South Dakota State University, earning a degree in chemistry and dairy science in 1932.

Ben Reifel

In 1933, Reifel served as a farm extension agent for the Pine Ridge Reservation, and in 1935, he worked to help the Sioux improve their business skills. While he was in college, Reifel had joined the U.S. Army reserves, and during World War II, he was called to duty. He served from 1942 to 1946. Before and after the war, he worked for the Bureau of Indian Affairs (BIA).

Following the war, he became the superintendent for the Fort Berthold Reservation. After receiving a scholarship to Harvard, though, he left to pursue his master's and doctoral degrees. Reifel wrote his dissertation on how to reduce conflict between Native Americans and non-Natives, a subject that was to be his project, years later, in Congress.

After completing his Ph.D., in 1952, Reifel went back to work for the BIA. In 1954, he became the first Native American superintendent of the Pine Ridge Reservation. The following year, he became an area director for the BIA. Not long after he became director, Reifel ran for Congress. He was elected and served for ten years.

In Congress, he pushed for better education on reservations and recommended that reservation and county schools be merged so that Native Americans and non-Natives could go to school together. He also helped to push through improvements to the Sioux Falls veterans' hospital and establish the National Endowment for the Humanities.

After retiring from Congress, Reifel returned to public service as the nation's last Commissioner of Indian Affairs, which, until 1977, was the head of the Bureau of Indian Affairs. The following year, the BIA was restructured to give it a stronger voice in the Department of the Interior. Since then, the head of the BIA has held the title of Assistant Secretary—Indian Affairs. Reifel died of cancer in 1990.

63. Annie Dodge Wauneka
(1910–1997)

The first Native American to receive the Presidential Medal of Freedom, Annie Dodge Wauneka worked tirelessly to stop the spread of tuberculosis on the Navajo Reservation.

The daughter of Henry Chee Dodge (see no. 47), Wauneka grew up on the Navajo Reservation. When she was eight years old, her father sent her to boarding school at Fort Defiance, Arizona. Soon after she arrived, many students died during a flu epidemic. Wauneka contracted a mild case and recovered. Then, she helped the school's only nurse care for the sick students. Annie never forgot how her classmates suffered while they were ill.

From the fifth through the eleventh grade, she attended the Albuquerque Indian School. When she returned home, she told her family she was going to marry George Wauneka, departing from the Navajo custom of arranged marriages. Her family, however, did not object. The couple, who eventually had nine children, established a division of labor that was unusual for their day. George stayed home to care

Annie Dodge Wauneka

for the children and a large herd of sheep. Annie traveled with her father, who apparently was training her to enter politics.

As Wauneka traveled, she observed that most Navajo were poor and had no electricity or running water in their homes. She also noted that diseases tended to spread rapidly on the reservation. What she learned spurred her desire to improve the living conditions of her people.

After her father died, Wauneka became the first woman elected to the Navajo Tribal Council, where she was to serve for nearly thirty years. She became the chair of the Council's Health and Welfare Committee, and a few years later, she joined the U.S. Advisory Committee on Indian Health.

In her role as a health advocate, Wauneka worked to eradicate tuberculosis, a highly contagious disease. Until the 1950s, tuberculosis was the leading cause of death in Western countries, but then doctors discovered antibiotics that could be used to treat it.

Wauneka studied tuberculosis at U.S. Public Health Service laboratories and then explained the new findings to Navajo leaders, who were suspicious of Anglo doctors. Wauneka even made up Navajo words for Western medical procedures to calm fearful patients.

She is credited with saving the lives of at least two thousand tuberculosis victims and with convincing twenty thousand Navajos to be screened for the disease. She also carried out a crusade to improve health conditions on the reservation, hosting a weekly radio show on health and sanitation.

In 1963, U.S. president John F. Kennedy chose Wauneka to receive the Presidential Medal of Freedom award. U.S. president Lyndon B. Johnson presented her with the award after Kennedy was assassinated. She continued to work to improve health conditions on the reservation until her death, in 1997.

Elizabeth Peratrovich spent much of her life working as an advocate for civil rights for Alaska Natives, and she was instrumental in the passage of Alaska's first antidiscrimination legislation.

Her parents died when she was very young. She was then adopted, becoming Elizabeth Wanamaker. She grew up in southeast Alaska and went to college in Bellingham, in Washington state. There, she met and married Roy Peratrovich.

In 1941, the Peratrovichs decided to move back to Roy's home, Klawock, Alaska. Later, they moved to Juneau, Alaska, where they were shocked by the racist environment they found. Klawock was a small Tlingit fishing community. Juneau was the territorial capital—Alaska was not yet a state—and the site of a gold rush. It had experienced an influx of white immigrants. Juneau businesses had posted signs reading, "We Cater to Whites Only," and "No Dogs or Natives Allowed."

Both the Peratrovichs became civil rights activists. Elizabeth became president of the Alaska Native Sisterhood (ANS), and Roy became president of the Alaska Native Brotherhood (ANB). The organizations advocated equal rights for Native Alaskans.

By 1945, Territorial Governor Ernest Gruening and Representative Anthony Diamond had managed to push an antidiscrimination bill through the territorial House of Representatives. In the Senate, though, the bill faced stiff opposition. Senator Allen Shattuck remarked, "Who are these people, barely out of savagery, who want to associate with us whites with five thousand years of recorded civilization behind us?"

When the floor was opened to public comment, Elizabeth Peratrovich faced the mostly white, mostly male, somewhat hostile crowd.

Elizabeth Peratrovich (second from left)

She said calmly, "I would not have expected that I, who am barely out of savagery, would have to remind gentlemen with five thousand years of civilization behind them of our Bill of Rights." She went on to describe the realities of discrimination, remaining steadfast during two hours of aggressive questioning. At one point, Senator Shattuck called out, "Will this law eliminate discrimination?" Peratrovich countered, "Do your laws against larceny, rape, and murder prevent those crimes?"

At her response, the gallery erupted with tears and applause. Senatorial opposition to the bill crumbled. It passed, eleven to five, making it illegal for Alaskan businesses to refuse equal accommodations on the basis of race.

Peratrovich spent the rest of her life working on behalf of civil rights for Native Alaskans. She pushed especially hard to achieve integration in Alaska's schools, and she continued to lead the ANS, becoming the representative to the National Congress of American Indians for both the ANB and the ANS.

Her civil rights work was done as a volunteer. During most of these years, she actually earned her income working in the offices of the Territorial Treasurer and the Territorial Vocational Rehabilitation Director. Peratrovich died of cancer, in 1958.

Howard Rock

As the first Inupiat newspaper editor, Howard Rock helped organize Native Alaskan political organizations, and he used his newspaper to help persuade the U.S. Congress to work toward a settlement of Alaska Native land claims.

Rock was born in 1911, in Point Hope, an ancient village on the north coast of present-day Alaska. As a young man, he studied art at the University of Washington. Then, he worked as an artist, carving ivory and designing jewelry. During World War II, he served in the U.S. Army Air Force.

Rock began his career as a community activist in 1961. He and other Inupiats discovered Project Chariot, a plan by the U.S. Atomic Energy Commission (AEC) to detonate several atomic bombs to create an artificial harbor near Point Hope. The AEC had not bothered to tell the local Inupiat, but it had already scheduled the explosion to take place in 1962. Rock spearheaded opposition to Project Chariot, and because of the outcry

from the Inupiat and environmental groups, the project was canceled.

Realizing the vulnerability of their land claims, Rock and other Inupiat leaders met in November 1961 and decided to create a statewide newspaper representing Alaska Natives. Rock was to be the editor. Two years later, Athabascan leaders from Alaska's interior organized their own association, the Tanana Chiefs Conference. The group mobilized to prevent the government from building a huge hydroelectric dam that would have flooded several villages.

In 1964, Rock organized a conference that brought together leaders from various Native associations in Alaska. They planned ways to coordinate their efforts to get legal recognition for Alaska Native land claims, and in 1966, they decided to form an umbrella organization, the Alaska Federation of Natives (AFN).

In 1968, oil was discovered at Prudhoe Bay, on Alaska's North Slope, and oil companies planned to build a pipeline from the Arctic Ocean to Prince William Sound. The AFN realized that the time had come to settle their land claims. The same year, a federal study confirmed that Alaska Natives had a valid claim to Alaska lands, which they had never signed away by treaty.

The AFN convinced Secretary of the Interior Stewart Udall to freeze the transfer of Alaska lands until land claims were settled. For several years, the AFN worked with Congress to hammer out a land claims bill, and Rock covered each stage of the fight in the *Tundra Times*. For this work, he was nominated for a Pulitzer Prize a few years later.

In 1971, Congress passed the Alaska Native Claims Settlement Act (ANCSA). It created thirteen Alaska Native regional corporations, which were given title to 44 million acres (17.8 million ha) of land and more than nine hundred million dollars.

Jay Silverheels was known to a generation of television viewers as Tonto, the Lone Ranger's faithful sidekick in the television show *The Lone Ranger*. Silverheels is also remembered for working hard to improve Hollywood's portrayal of his people. He served as a mentor to other Native American actors.

Silverheels was born Harold Smith on the Six Nations Reservation in Ontario, Canada. His father was a leader of the Mohawk, one of the nations of the Iroquois Confederacy. During the first decades of his life, Silverheels was a champion lacrosse player in Canada, and he won awards in several other sports as well.

In 1938, touring with Canada's national lacrosse team, Silverheels traveled to the United States. There, he met comedian Joe E. Brown, who encouraged him to begin acting and paved the way for him to begin working as a stuntman. Except for a stint in the military during World War II, Silverheels played minor roles in western movies for the next nine years.

In 1947, Silverheels landed his first important film role, an Aztec warrior in *The Captain from Castille*. His performance attracted attention from several directors and producers. Two years later, he was cast in the part of Tonto in *The Lone Ranger*, a television show based on a hit radio series. The Tonto character helped the Lone Ranger fight for law and order in the American West. Silverheels viewed the role as a chance to depict Native Americans in a more positive way than Hollywood normally did.

Silverheels continued to act in movies during the eight years he starred in *The Lone Ranger*. He appeared in more than thirty films, portraying such notable Native Americans as Little Crow, Red Cloud (see no. 29), and Geronimo (see no. 35). His performance as Geronimo in the 1950 movie *Broken Arrow* received rave reviews.

Many people believe that Silverheels helped change public perceptions of Native Americans, because he was most often cast as a "good guy." As often as possible, he deliberately chose to act in movies that showed Native Americans and people of European descent living together peacefully. He also spoke out against the practice of hiring white actors to play Native Americans.

During the 1960s, Silverheels founded the Indian Actors Workshop. He was a mentor to other Native American actors, helping them to advance their careers. He also worked on public service projects intended to decrease substance abuse and help the elderly.

In the course of his life, Silverheels made nearly sixty movies. In 1979, he became the first Native American to have a star placed in Hollywood's Walk of Fame. A year later, he died of pneumonia, and his ashes were scattered on the Six Nations Reservation in Canada.

Jay Silverheels

Oscar Howe was one of the first Native American artists to combine traditional and modern elements in his work.

Howe, who was born on South Dakota's Crow Creek Reservation, had a difficult childhood. Although his great-grandfather was a tribal historian who painted Sioux history on buffalo hides, Howe's parents discouraged him from drawing. At about the age of six, however, he developed a skin disease that caused open sores on his body. Other children did not want to play with him, and he spent much of his time alone, drawing.

When Howe turned seven, he was sent to the government Indian school in Pierre, South Dakota. He could not speak English and was often punished for speaking Sioux. His skin disease worsened, and he developed an eye disease as well. During this period, Howe's mother died. Miserable, he tried many times to run away from the school.

Fortunately, school authorities decided to send him home because of his health problems, and Howe's grandmother took charge of his education for a while. She taught him about the traditional art of the Dakota Sioux. Eventually, Howe returned to the school in Pierre. He graduated from eighth grade at the age of eighteen and began working as a laborer.

By the age of twenty, Howe had contracted tuberculosis. Told to move to a dry climate, he traveled to Santa Fe, New Mexico, to attend high school and study art. By the time he finished high school and recovered from his illness, his paintings were being exhibited across the United States and Europe.

After serving in the army during World War II, Howe became an artist-in-residence at Dakota Wesleyan University, where he earned his bachelor's degree. Howe then completed a master's in fine arts at the University of Oklahoma and accepted a job teaching at the University of South Dakota (USD).

At USD, Howe continued to paint. He combined the ideas of abstract art, cubism, and traditional Sioux art. Art dealers and critics, however, often rejected his art for "not looking Indian." The final straw for Howe came in 1958, when the Philbrook Indian Art Annual committee rejected a painting of his as "a fine painting—but not Indian."

Howe wrote an angry letter in response, stating, "Whoever said that my paintings are not in the traditional Indian style has poor knowledge of Indian art indeed. There is much more to Indian art than pretty, stylized pictures … "

His letter convinced the committee, and his paintings have convinced much of the art world as well. Howe paved the way for many Native American artists, who followed him to develop a variety of styles in their artwork.

Oscar Howe

Pablita Velarde became one of the most influential Native American artists of the twentieth century.

Velarde grew up at Santa Clara Pueblo, south of Santa Fe, New Mexico. When she was three years old, her mother died of tuberculosis. Soon afterward, an eye infection left Velarde blind. Her father treated her with herbs, and after two years, she regained her sight. From that point on, Velarde was hungry for visual details. "I wanted to see everything," she said later.

At the age of six, Velarde was sent to boarding school in Santa Fe. During the summers, she returned home, where her father and grandmother provided her with a Pueblo education. When Velarde turned fourteen, she entered the Santa Fe Indian School.

Previously, the school had discouraged Native American students from painting, but at about this time, the policy was changed. The school hired a famous art teacher, Dorothy Dunn, and Velarde became her only female student. Among the Pueblo, painting was traditionally a male activity. The boys in the classes ridiculed her, telling her to go to work in the school kitchen.

Velarde persevered, however, inspired partly by a visit from another Pueblo woman painter, Tonita Peña. When Velarde had been painting for only a year, her work was exhibited at the Museum of New Mexico. In 1933, Santa Fe artist Olive Rush invited Velarde to help paint a mural for the Works Progress Administration (WPA), a federal program that created jobs through public works projects during the Depression.

In 1936, Velarde graduated and began teaching and painting in Santa Clara. She also briefly worked as a nanny for Edward Thompson Seton, the founder of the Boy Scouts. This job gave her the opportunity to travel and to exhibit and sell some of her paintings.

In 1938, the U.S. Park Service commissioned Velarde to do a series of murals about Pueblo life. First, Velarde interviewed elders and researched Pueblo history. She then painted murals containing so much detailed information that, today, they serve as archaeological sources for scholars.

At first Velarde used casein and tempera paints in her work. Later, she developed her own series of "earth colors," which she made herself by grinding rocks into powder and then mixing them with water and glue. Using these paints, Velarde was able to paint textured pictures like those often found on the walls of ancient Pueblo kivas, the underground rooms used for special ceremonies.

Velarde's work has won many awards and has made her internationally famous. She also paved the way for other Pueblo women, including her own daughter, Helen Hardin, to become artists.

Pablita Velarde

Ira Hayes is best known as one of the U.S. Marines who raised the U.S. flag over Iwo Jima, an act of bravery captured in one of the most famous photographs of World War II.

Hayes was born on the Pima Reservation in Arizona. Little is known of his early life. When World War II began, Hayes, along with many thousands of other Native Americans, enlisted in the armed forces.

Hayes was trained as a paratrooper and served in several battles in the Pacific. In 1945, his division landed on Iwo Jima, a Japanese island that the United States hoped to use as a base for its fighter planes. Although the navy and air force tried to weaken Japanese resistance for weeks before the marines landed, Japanese soldiers fought vigorously, and the struggle to capture Iwo Jima lasted nearly a month.

Mount Suribachi, an extinct volcano, proved to be one of the hardest areas to conquer. Hayes and the others in his division fought for each short distance that they advanced. The soldiers finally reached the peak on February 23, 1945. Although Iwo Jima itself had not yet been captured, Hayes and five others erected a U.S. flag, as a symbol of their victory. A photographer named Joe Rosenthal captured the scene with a camera, and the resulting picture made Hayes and the others national heroes in the United States.

Of the soldiers in the picture, only Hayes and two others survived Iwo Jima. The three soldiers were flown home and welcomed by U.S. president Franklin D. Roosevelt. Then, they were given noncombat status and were assigned to sell war bonds. Everywhere they went, they were honored with parades, receptions, and, often, free alcohol. The constant adulation disturbed Hayes, who believed he had done no more for the United States than any other soldier. Once, he said he wished "that guy had never made that picture."

Hayes requested permission to return to combat, but the war was nearly over. He finished his tour of duty with the marines and then went home to the Pima Reservation, but his celebrity made him feel out of place. He started to move around the country, taking jobs that never lasted very long. Everywhere he went, people offered Hayes free drinks in honor of his war service, and he rarely refused them. Eventually, he became an alcoholic.

Over a period of thirteen years, Hayes was arrested more than fifty times, always for drinking-related offenses that usually began with well-wishers pressing him to accept free drinks. Finally, after his last drinking binge, Hayes passed out and died of exposure in the Arizona desert. He was remembered as "a hero to everyone but himself."

Ira Hayes

Betty Mae Tiger Jumper
(1923–)

Betty Mae Tiger Jumper became the first Seminole woman, and the first Native American woman in North America, to be the leader of her nation.

Jumper first began overcoming adversity as a child. At the time, some Seminoles in her community made a practice of drowning babies of mixed descent at birth, and Jumper was the daughter of a Seminole mother and a white father. Her family chose not to drown her or her younger brother, but when she was five years old, a group of Seminole men came to her home and demanded that she and her then two-year-old brother be killed. Jumper's great-uncle, who was a Seminole religious leader, drove them away.

Soon afterward, for safety reasons, the family moved from their home in Indiantown, Florida, near Lake Okeechobee, to Dania Indian Reservation, near Fort Lauderdale, Florida. Her mother became a field worker, picking beans and tomatoes. Jumper and her brother helped.

The Seminole were determined to avoid being assimilated into mainstream U.S. culture, and they deliberately avoided white schools. Jumper's grandparents discouraged her from learning to read. One day, however, Jumper found a comic book at church. (Her family had been the first Seminole converts to Christianity.) The comic book sparked her determination to attend school.

At the age of fourteen, Jumper persuaded her family to let her attend a boarding school for Native Americans, nearly 1,000 miles (1,600 km) away in North Carolina. Eight years later, she and her cousin became the first Seminoles to graduate from high school.

Jumper was not finished with her education. Recalling how frequently Seminole children died of treatable diseases such as whooping cough, she moved to Oklahoma and went to nursing school. She became the first Seminole

Betty Mae Tiger Jumper

nurse, and like Annie Dodge Wauneka (see no. 63), she worked tirelessly to improve health conditions on reservations.

In 1957, the Seminole nation put together a charter formally establishing its status as a political authority. Jumper was elected as a representative to the Seminole Tribal Council in the first formal election. She continued to work on the council throughout the 1960s, eventually being elected as its chairperson. As a politician, Jumper worked to improve the health, education, and housing of Seminoles. She also became a founding member of the United Southeastern Tribes (USET), a regional network including the Seminole, Cherokee, Choctaw, and other nations.

Jumper left office in 1971 and became the director for Seminole Communications, which publishes the *Seminole Tribune*. She has also narrated stories at cultural events and folklore festivals, and in the 1990s, she produced a video depicting several Seminole stories. In 1995, Jumper was inducted into the Florida Women's Hall of Fame.

Celilo Falls on the Columbia River

David Sohappy, a Yakima fisherman, was an important figure in the struggle to maintain the fishing rights of Native Americans in the Northwest.

Sohappy was the grandson of Smohalla, a Wanapam prophet who founded the Dreamer religion. Dreamers try to follow ancient practices and avoid being corrupted by European-American culture. Dreamers also believe that the Earth provides everything they need to live, especially salmon.

Sohappy, who was a Dreamer, only attended school through fourth grade, because his family believed reading and writing were the only useful things one could learn in a white school. As a young man, he served in the U.S. Army during World War II. After his discharge, he worked in a sawmill for awhile. When he was laid off, he and his family moved to Cook's Landing, Washington, a temporary fishing camp alongside the Columbia River.

At Cook's Landing, Sohappy built a longhouse and fishing traps. The Yakima had lived along the Columbia River for thousands of years, and many families there refused to go to reservations. As a matter of religion and law, Sohappy maintained that the Yakima had a right to live next to the Columbia River and fish there. In fact, an 1855 treaty guaranteed the Yakima and other nations that right.

Cook's Landing, however, was only a temporary camp. The camp was created when the government flooded Celilo, a Native village, in order to make a dam. Celilo had been protected under the 1855 treaty.

In 1968, state and federal fish and game officials raided Sohappy's home and arrested him for illegal fishing. He then took his case, *Sohappy v. Smith*, to court. The result was a landmark U.S. District Court ruling that the 1855 treaty rights were still valid. The judge stated that Native Americans had a right to a "fair and equitable" share of the fish, and later rulings established this share to be 50 percent of Columbia River salmon.

State officials disagreed. Over the next twenty years, they confiscated 230 of Sohappy's nets and often tried to evict the family from their home. In 1983, federal officials trapped Sohappy and his son in a sting operation called "Salmonscam." Both were arrested, convicted of selling fish out of season, and sent to a federal prison to serve five years. After a public outcry, Sohappy's lawyer was able to get his case retried in tribal court, and Sohappy was released after twenty months.

Sohappy had suffered several strokes in prison, however, and his health was failing. Returning home to find another eviction notice tacked to his door, Sohappy went back to court and won his last case. He moved to a nursing home in Hood River, Oregon, where he died in 1991.

Maria Tallchief
(1925–)

Ballet aficionados consider Maria Tallchief to be the greatest American prima ballerina of all time. She is the first American ballerina to become internationally famous.

Tallchief was the daughter of an Osage father and a mother who was Dutch, Scottish, and Irish. About twenty years before Tallchief was born, oil was discovered on Oklahoma's Osage Reservation. Many Osage, including Tallchief's family, became wealthy by leasing their land to oil-drilling companies. Tallchief's parents could afford to provide their daughter with music and dance lessons from the time she was a toddler. Tallchief, who was called Betty Marie as a child, could play the piano and dance ballet positions by the time she was four years old.

When Tallchief was eight, she and her family moved to Beverly Hills, California. In addition to dancing, she also began to study music and considered becoming a concert pianist. As a teenager, however, she decided to concentrate on ballet instead.

In 1942, she joined the Ballet Russe de Monte Carlo. The company asked her to change her name to "Tallchieva," to make her sound Russian. At the time, many ballet fans believed only Russians and Europeans could dance well. Tallchief refused, but she did change her first name to Maria.

George Balanchine, who was to become the most important ballet choreographer in the United States in the twentieth century, took over the ballet troupe in 1944. He admired Tallchief, who danced the lead in many of his ballets. In 1946, the two were married, but the marriage only lasted a few years. The following year, Tallchief was invited to dance at the Paris Opera, becoming the first American ballerina to dance there in 108 years. Some European reporters gossiped that she must really be French or Russian. Others imagined her to be an "Indian princess."

Leaving Paris, Tallchief joined Balanchine's new company, the New York City Ballet. Balanchine choreographed his ballets to showcase Tallchief's speed and athleticism. After she danced the lead in *Firebird*, critics described her as having an "almost frightening technical range," and her success made her internationally famous. In the following years, she danced many of her most famous roles, including *Swan Lake*, *Serenade*, *Scotch Symphony*, and *The Nutcracker*. In 1953, the Osage Tribal Council honored her, and the Oklahoma State Senate declared June 29 "Maria Tallchief Day."

Later in her life, Tallchief directed a corps of dancers for the Chicago Lyric Opera. She founded the Chicago City Ballet in 1980. In 1996, Tallchief was awarded a Kennedy Center Honors award for Lifetime Achievement, the most prestigious performing arts award in the United States.

Maria Tallchief

LaDonna Harris

Organizer and activist LaDonna Harris has spent her life working to protect the rights of Native Americans. She has also become involved in the feminist and peace movements.

Harris was born in Temple, Oklahoma, to a Comanche mother and an Irish-American father. Her parents separated shortly after her birth because of the discrimination they faced as a mixed-race couple. Harris was raised by her Comanche grandparents. Her grandmother was a Christian and her grandfather was a traditional healer, but they respected each other's beliefs and raised Harris to respect the beliefs of others. Harris spoke only Comanche until she began attending public school at the age of six. She attended an integrated school, and children on the bus taunted her about being an Indian.

In high school, LaDonna met Fred Harris, the son of a poor white sharecropper, and the two were married soon after he entered college. LaDonna put her career on hold while she worked to support her husband's education and to bring up their three children. After Fred became a U.S. senator from Oklahoma, LaDonna began to pursue her own interests.

In 1965, at a time when the country was caught up in the African American Civil Rights Movement, Harris was working to end segregation of Native Americans in Oklahoma. She worked with sixty of the state's Native nations and organized the state's first intertribal organization, Oklahomans for Indian Opportunity.

By this time, Harris had become a nationally known activist. In 1967, U.S. president Lyndon Johnson appointed her the chairperson of the National Women's Advisory Council of the War on Poverty. Later, he appointed her to the National Council on Indian Opportunity (NCIO), a council that he created.

When Richard Nixon became U.S. president in 1969, he placed the NCIO on the back burner, and Harris resigned. She then helped found the National Women's Political Caucus. In 1970, she founded Americans for Indian Opportunity, and she became its first president. AIO works to strengthen tribal governments. It has also created a national computer network called INDIANnet, a resource dedicated to making the Internet accessible to Native Americans.

In recent years, Harris has become an important peace activist. U.S. president Jimmy Carter encouraged her to form a Native American version of the Peace Corps, called the "Peace Pipe Project." She found that indigenous people in other countries felt comfortable working with indigenous people from the Americas, and the Peace Pipe workers learned skills that helped them find better jobs when they returned to the United States. In the twenty-first century, Harris continued to work with the AIO and served on the boards of many nonprofit organizations.

Louis Ballard is one of the most popular contemporary Native American composers. His work is performed by philharmonic orchestras and ballet companies across the United States and Europe.

Ballard was born in northeast Oklahoma, the son of a Quapaw-French mother and a Cherokee-Scot father. During his youth, he spent time with his grandmother on the reservation and with his mother and stepfather in European-American communities. In both environments, music surrounded him.

At tribal ceremonials, Ballard learned Quapaw songs and dances. His mother, a pianist, wrote children's songs. Ballard's grandmother encouraged him to take piano lessons. Soon after he began to learn the piano, Ballard started to compose his own music. He also grew interested in the music of other Native American nations.

As a young adult, Ballard studied music at the University of Tulsa, where he earned a bachelor's degree. To finance his education, he worked as a janitor, dishwasher, ambulance driver, and waiter, as well as a nightclub pianist and singer. The focus of Ballard's early formal musical training was classical music, and he especially admired the Hungarian composer Béla Bartók.

Bartók incorporated Hungarian folk music into his compositions, and Ballard was inspired to incorporate Native American themes into his own work. Many European composers had written instrumental works based on their perception of Native Americans, but Ballard felt these works were not authentic. He believed classical composers could learn from Native American harmonies and instruments and incorporate them into their works.

To this end, Ballard began collecting music from many Native American traditions. Determined to bring Native music into the mainstream, he composed ballets, chamber music, orchestral variations, and choral arrangements inspired by Native music and using Native American instruments.

In 1960, he wrote a ballet, *Koshare*, based on a Hopi creation story. In 1969, he won an award for his woodwind quartet *Ritmo Indio*, which replaces the usual oboe with a Lakota instrument similar to a flute. Ballard has also written works based on historical incidents or real people, such as *Incident at Wounded Knee* and *Portrait of Will*, a cantata based on the life of Will Rogers (see no. 54). Symphony orchestras, ballet companies, and choirs have performed his works frequently.

In addition to composing his own music, Ballard has worked to bring Native American music to young music students across the country. In the 1970s, he served as the music department dean for the Institute of American Indian Arts in Santa Fe, New Mexico, and as the music curriculum specialist for the Bureau of Indian Affairs. Over the years, he has also worked with reservation schools to make it possible for students to use Native instruments and learn the cultural context for Native American music.

Louis Ballard

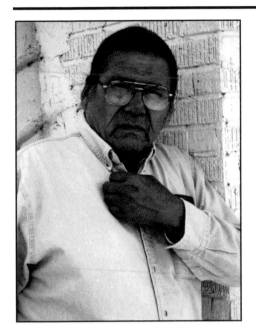

Dennis Banks

Dennis Banks was one of the founders of the American Indian Movement (AIM), an organization that works to defend Native American civil rights.

Banks was born on the Leech Lake Reservation, an Ojibwa reservation in northern Minnesota. He was taken from his family at the age of five and sent to a Bureau of Indian Affairs (BIA) boarding school.

In 1953, Banks joined the U.S. Air Force and was sent to Japan. After he returned home, he drifted from one city to another, unable to find a job. In 1966, he went to prison for burglary. After his release, he met with Clyde Bellecourt (see no. 85), George Mitchell, and Eddie Banai, ex-convicts who were concerned about the lack of jobs, education, and housing for urban Native Americans. Together, they founded the American Indian Movement.

At first, Banks and Bellecourt organized street patrols, filming arrests of Native Americans and informing arrestees of their legal rights. Banks and Bellecourt were often beaten up by police and jailed. Later, they put together a program for mothers of juvenile offenders to report on racism within the juvenile court system. They also worked with public school systems to get rid of racist textbooks. Then, they founded schools of their own, where Native students could learn about their heritage.

In the early 1970s, AIM became known for its dramatic political protests, such as the occupation of Alcatraz prison and the Trail of Broken Treaties, a march on Washington, D.C. In 1973, Banks, Bellecourt, and other AIM activists took over the village of Wounded Knee and proclaimed it the "Independent Oglala Nation," partly because of Wounded Knee's historical significance and partly because local elders had asked for their help. Soon, they were surrounded by FBI agents, U.S. marshals, and the BIA police. Federal officials laid siege to the village, occasionally exchanging fire with the activists. After seventy-one days of negotiations, the activists agreed to allow themselves to be arrested.

Banks was acquitted of the Wounded Knee charges, but he was convicted of charges stemming from an earlier protest. He escaped to California, however, where Governor Jerry Brown offered him amnesty. In California, he began teaching. When Brown's term as governor ended, New York's Onondaga nation offered Banks refuge. Instead, in 1984, he surrendered to authorities and served an eighteen-month prison sentence. Afterward, he returned to the Pine Ridge Reservation to work as a drug and alcohol counselor.

In the late 1980s, Banks published his autobiography, *Sacred Soul*, in Japan. He has also starred in several films. In 2001, at the age of sixty-nine, he returned to the Leech Lake Reservation and started his own wild rice and maple syrup company.

76. Fred Begay
(1932–)

The first Navajo ever to earn a Ph.D. in physics, Fred Begay has won many awards for his service to the Navajo nation and for mentoring young minority science students.

Begay was born at Towaoc, Colorado, on the Ute Mountain Indian Reservation. His parents, who were both Navajo and Ute, were traditional Navajo healers. Begay grew up speaking both Navajo and Ute. When Begay was six years old, his parents began training him to practice Navajo medicine, starting with the songs of the Blessing Way ceremony.

When he was ten, he began to attend a Bureau of Indian Affairs boarding school. Like most of these schools, the one Begay attended prohibited students from speaking their own languages or attending Native American religious ceremonies. The school trained students to become farmers. "They thought we weren't intelligent enough for academic learning," Begay remembers.

At the age of nineteen, Begay still had not graduated from high school, and he joined the U.S. Army Air Corps and served in the Korean War. Returning home, he married and set about raising children and running a farm. The Navajo nation, however, was recruiting war veterans to go to college. Begay enrolled at the University of New Mexico. The school accepted him with the understanding that he would get his high school diploma, but he never did. Sixteen years, seven children, and a doctorate in nuclear physics later, he was offered a job at Los Alamos National Laboratory.

Many people have questioned how Begay was able to finish a doctorate in nuclear physics without having ever completed high school. The answer is that his early Navajo math and science training served him well. Navajo math uses base-8 arithmetic, just like computer science and fractal geometry. Navajo weavers use complex geometric designs in their weaving, and Navajo science includes versions of the concepts of gravity, fusion energy, solar radiation, and even the modern gas discharge laser.

Although Los Alamos is famous for being the place where the first atom bomb was developed, Begay's work is in other areas. He hopes to find an alternative energy source, joining atoms to give off heat. In addition to his work at Los Alamos, he frequently advises the Navajo nation about science and technology, and he takes the time to teach science classes to middle school Navajo students.

In 1999, Begay won the Distinguished Scientist Award from the Society for the Advancement of Chicanos and Native Americans in Science. Begay is also the head of the Seaborg Hall of Science, an organization that provides science and technology-related services, especially education, to people in the Navajo community.

Fred Begay

(1933–)

Ben Nighthorse Campbell

In 1992, Northern Cheyenne chief Ben Nighthorse Campbell became the first Native American to serve in the United States Senate in more than sixty years.

Campbell had a very difficult upbringing. His father was an alcoholic, and his mother suffered from tuberculosis. He and his sister sometimes lived in orphanages, and they lived briefly with their mother in a sanitarium, where she had been institutionalized for her health. The family was very poor. Campbell remembers one evening when his mother opened a can of peas, gave the peas to the children, and then drank the juice for her own dinner. When he was growing up, Campbell later remarked, "becoming a U.S. senator was just about the last thing I imagined."

Like many kids who grow up in rough circumstances, Campbell dropped out of school.

He joined the U.S. Air Force and served in the Korean War. He also completed a GED high school diploma. He later said that the military gave his life predictability, structure, and a regular income—three things that had been lacking during his youth. Campbell turned to sports as an escape. He studied martial arts, becoming one of the youngest Americans to hold a fourth-degree black belt in judo. In 1964, he captained the U.S. judo team at the Summer Olympics in Tokyo.

When Campbell returned from Korea, he attended San Jose State University, where he studied physical education and fine arts. Later, he attended Meiji University, in Tokyo. He also began to work as a jewelry designer, using the name Ben Nighthorse. His designs have won more than two hundred awards.

In 1982, Campbell entered politics and was elected to the Colorado State Legislature. In 1987, he moved on to the U.S. House of Representatives, becoming, as he said, "the only member of Congress who goes to work on a motorcycle." In 1992, he decided to run for the U.S. Senate, and he won. He became the first Native American ever to chair the Senate's Indian Affairs Committee.

Campbell has also served on other important committees, related to energy and natural resource management. He has worked hard to pass legislation settling Native American water rights and protecting Colorado's wilderness areas. In addition, he has led the battle to prevent fetal alcohol syndrome, the birth defects that afflict babies born to mothers who drink alcohol during pregnancy.

In 1995, Campbell shocked political observers by switching from the Democratic party to the Republican party. He said at the time that he felt the Democratic party had been taken over by special interests. In 1998, running as a Republican, Campbell was reelected to another term.

Vine Deloria Jr.
(1933–2005)

Historian and activist Vine Deloria Jr. was one of the founders of Native American studies as a scholarly field.

Deloria was born to a distinguished Sioux family. His great-grandfather was a Sioux healer, and his grandfather was an Episcopal missionary. His aunt Ella Deloria (see no. 60) was a famous ethnographer, and his father was the first Native American to be named to a national position in the Episcopal church. As a young boy during the 1930s, Deloria grew up listening to veterans of the Battle of the Little Bighorn tell stories about that famous battle.

At first, Deloria considered following in his father's footsteps as a minister. After a brief stint in the U.S. Marine Corps, from 1954 to 1956, he earned a degree from Iowa State University, and then he attended Augustana Lutheran Seminary. He went on to earn a master's degree in sacred theology and began working for United Scholarship Service, a church group.

In 1959, Deloria became the executive director for the National Congress of American Indians (NCAI), and he worked to prevent various Native nations from having their tribal recognition terminated. Deloria began to realize that many Native nations did not have lawyers. He again returned to school, this time completing a law degree. While attending law school, he wrote his first book, *Custer Died for Your Sins*, which became known as an "Indian rights manifesto."

After completing his degree, Deloria and his family moved to Washington state, where they became involved with the struggle for Puyallup and Nisqually fishing rights. He also taught college classes. Using his legal training, Deloria wrote books, such as *Of Utmost Good Faith* and *Behind the Trail of Broken Treaties*, documenting the treaties, acts, and rulings that affect Native Americans. He also helped to defend American Indian Movement (AIM) leaders during their trial for the occupation of Wounded Knee.

Deloria continued to write books that presented an activist viewpoint on Native American issues. His book *We Talk, You Listen* was called an "American Indian Declaration of Independence." His writing often touched upon religious themes, and his 1973 book, *God Is Red*, shocked the nation with its indictment of Christianity's role in Native American genocides. In his 1995 book, *Red Earth, White Lies,* he tried to refute the theory that Native Americans first came to the Americas via the Bering Strait land bridge 15,000 years ago by claiming that they actually lived in North America as early as 200,000 years ago.

In recent years, in addition to his own scholarship, Deloria planned conferences to recover and preserve ancient Native American scientific knowledge. At the conferences, elders exchanged knowledge about their nation's pre-Columbian understanding of the stars, farming techniques, and animals.

Vine Deloria Jr.

Janet McCloud
(1934–2003)

Janet McCloud helped establish at least five Native American activist organizations.

A descendant of Chief Seathl (see no. 18), McCloud was born on Washington's Tulalip Reservation. As a child, she was left alone with her younger sisters and cousins while her alcoholic mother and stepfather went out drinking. Meanwhile, drunks from the neighborhood would come into the house and abuse her and the other children. By the time McCloud was seven years old, she had taught the older children to defend the younger ones, using axes and knives to drive the drunks out of the house. McCloud has said, "So, that was my first organizing."

McCloud wound up living in foster homes. She had low self-esteem, and she tried to commit suicide at age twelve. She married very young and was soon divorced. Then, she married Don McCloud. The couple began living off the land.

In the 1960s, McCloud hoped to organize the Tulalip and the Nisqually to develop their own fisheries. The state of Washington, however, did not recognize Native fishing rights guaranteed by treaties. In 1961, state authorities arrested several Nisqually fishermen. The state insisted it had a right to regulate fisheries and accused Native fishermen of depleting the salmon population by overfishing.

Along with women such as Ramona Bennett (see no. 84), McCloud kept a vigil in fishing boats, in what would later become known as "fish-ins." She and her husband founded the Survival of American Indian Association to fight state policies, and she began publishing the association's newsletter, *Survival News.* The fish-ins continued, and McCloud and her family were sometimes arrested.

Comedian Dick Gregory arrived to support the protesters and was arrested. He began fasting in jail. McCloud put up a tepee across from the jail. She told police that, since the state would not keep treaties with Northwest Natives, she was reclaiming the land.

The fishing rights activists eventually succeeded, to some extent. The courts ruled that Native Americans in Washington had a right to half of the fish caught in coastal waters.

The fish-ins were not the end of McCloud's activism. In the early 1970s, she worked with the Native American Rights Fund (NARF) and founded the Brotherhood of American Prisoners. Later, she helped organize Women of All Red Nations (WARN), a sister group to the American Indian Movement (AIM), and the Northwest Indian Women's Circle.

McCloud also built a lodge called the Sapa Dawn Center, dedicated to the pursuit of justice for indigenous families. In 1985, women from several countries met there with McCloud and formed the Indigenous Women's Network, an organization that advocates the sovereignty of Native nations in the Americas. McCloud died in 2003.

Janet McCloud

N. Scott Momaday

In the 1960s, N. Scott Momaday began a Native American literary renaissance when his book, *House Made of Dawn*, made him the first Native American writer to win the Pulitzer Prize for fiction.

A Kiowa, Momaday lived on the Kiowa Reservation in Oklahoma for the first two years of his life. Then, his parents accepted teaching jobs on reservations in Arizona. Momaday grew up in the Southwest, exposed not only to his own Kiowa traditions but also to the Navajo, Apache, and Pueblo cultures.

Momaday's father was a painter, and his mother was a writer who loved English literature. She so influenced the imaginative young Momaday that, as a child, he thought he saw the shadow of Grendel, a monster from the epic poem *Beowolf*, on the wall of the Canyon de Chelly.

For most of his childhood, Momaday attended school on reservations in Arizona and New Mexico. He also attended a Virginia military academy for a year. After graduating, he attended the University of New Mexico and then taught school for a year on the Jicarilla Apache Reservation. Then, he won a fellowship to Stanford University, where he entered a doctoral program in American literature. After leaving Stanford, he taught at the University of California, Santa Barbara.

House Made of Dawn was Momaday's first novel. It was published in 1968. The story of a Native American veteran adjusting to life after World War II, the book earned the Pulitzer Prize and made Momaday famous. The next year, he moved to the University of California at Berkeley and published *The Way to Rainy Mountain*, a work many critics have called his greatest. While at Berkeley, Momaday didn't confine himself to writing. He also designed a graduate program in Indian Studies, and he taught courses in American Indian literature and mythology.

Momaday is famous for his novels, which include *The Names* and *The Ancient Child*, but he thinks of himself as more of a poet than a novelist. He has published several collections of poetry, and he received the Academy of American Poets prize in 1962 for "The Bear."

In an interview, Momaday noted that people pay more attention to novels, but that he considers poetry the "highest form of expression." He expresses himself as a visual artist, too. In 1974, he began to draw and paint, finally pursuing his father's interest in the visual arts. His works have been exhibited throughout the United States, and contemporary editions of his books often include his own illustrations.

At the turn of the twenty-first century, Momaday began organizing a project called "The Buffalo Trust," which is dedicated to preserving Native culture for future generations.

Menominee activist Ada Deer led a movement to restore her people's status as a federally recognized tribe, and she later became the first woman to head the Bureau of Indian Affairs (BIA).

Deer grew up on the Menominee Reservation in northern Wisconsin. Until she turned eighteen, she lived with her family, which included her Menominee father, white mother, and four younger siblings, in a one-room log cabin with no heat or running water.

Deer's mother impressed upon her, at an early age, that she had a duty to help her people, and it became a lifelong effort on her part. She earned a bachelor's degree in social work from the University of Wisconsin, Madison, becoming its first Menominee graduate. Then, she became the first Native American to earn a master's degree in social work from Columbia University. She briefly attended the University of Wisconsin, Madison, Law School, but she left to help the Menominee, whose plight was becoming urgent.

In 1954, Congress had terminated the Menominee's status as a federally recognized tribe, believing they were prosperous enough to survive without federal assistance. The government schools and reservation hospital were shut down, the land became subject to taxation, and the tribal membership rolls were closed. Soon, their leaders were selling land in a desperate attempt to raise money.

In 1970, Deer joined other Menominees in forming Determination of the Rights and Unity of Menominee Shareholders, or DRUMS. She also became the vice-president of the National Committee to Save the Menominee People and Forest, and she traveled to Washington, D.C., to persuade the U.S. Congress to reinstate the Menominee as a tribe. In 1973, U.S. president Richard Nixon signed the Menominee Restoration Act. This act was a historical reversal of American Indian policy, and it set an important precedent for other tribes.

Deer was elected the chairperson of the newly formed Menominee government. After ushering through a transition period, she resigned. For fifteen years, she taught at the University of Wisconsin, Madison. During the 1980s and 1990s, she returned to politics, making two unsuccessful bids for Wisconsin Secretary of State and one for Congress.

In 1993, U.S. president Bill Clinton appointed Deer to head the Bureau of Indian Affairs, making her the first woman assistant secretary of the Department of the Interior.

Deer worked to give Native American nations more control over the BIA funds they received, while lobbying against those in Congress who wanted to reduce the BIA's budget. She left office in 1997 and returned to the University of Wisconsin, Madison, where she became director of American Indian Studies and distinguished lecturer at the School of Social Work.

Ada E. Deer

Peterson Zah led the efforts to reorganize the Navajo tribal government. In 1990, he became the last tribal chairman and the tribe's first elected president.

Zah grew up in Low Mountain, Arizona, in a disputed area of land called the Navajo-Hopi Joint Use Area. Both Navajo and Hopi lived in the area, and Zah grew comfortable with both cultures.

For years, the Bureau of Indian Affairs had a policy of separating Native American children from their families, often by force, and sending them to boarding schools, where teachers tried to make the children abandon their language and culture. When Zah was nine years old, he was taken from his family and sent to one of these boarding schools, in Phoenix, Arizona. Several years later, he attended Phoenix College, where he played basketball, and he graduated in 1960. He then transferred to Arizona State University, where he graduated in 1963 with a degree in education.

In 1967, Zah moved to Window Rock, Arizona, where he took a job as head of Dinébeiina Nahiilna Be Agaditahe (DNA). DNA provided legal assistance to Navajo, and, later, Hopi and Apache, whose annual income was under $3,500. Zah was involved in thousands of DNA cases, including some landmark decisions rendered by the U.S. Supreme Court. The job would be his stepping stone to politics.

Zah did not spend all of his time working for DNA. He also served on the first all-Navajo school board at Window Rock, and he became its president in 1973. He pushed the board to hire more Navajo teachers and to teach the Navajo language, culture, and history in the schools.

In 1978, many Navajo pressed Zah to run for tribal chairperson, but he waited until 1982 to take on incumbent Peter MacDonald. The Navajo-Hopi land dispute became an impor-

tant issue in the campaign. In 1974, Congress had passed an act that gave half of the land to the Hopi and required many Navajo and some Hopi to relocate to other areas. Zah stressed the importance of co-existence and of healing the damage done by the land dispute. He won the election, and he then began working with the Hopi people to resolve the dispute and reform the tribal government. In the next election, though, Zah narrowly lost to MacDonald.

MacDonald's administration, however, quickly fell apart. MacDonald was convicted of corruption and bribery in a tribal court, and then of conspiracy and assault in federal court, and he was sent to federal prison for fourteen years. Zah ran again in 1990 and, after winning, became the first president of the Navajo nation under the newly reorganized government structure. He held the position until 1995. That year, he became an advisor to the president on American Indian Affairs at Arizona State University.

Peterson Zah

Billy Mills became the first American athlete to win a gold medal in a long-distance track event at the Olympic Games.

Mills grew up on the Lakota's Pine Ridge Reservation in South Dakota, one of eight children. His mother died when he was six years old, and his father died when he was twelve. After his father died, Mills was sent to a Bureau of Indian Affairs boarding school, the Haskell Indian School, in Lawrence, Kansas.

As a member of the football team, Mills rejected track as a "sissy" sport. When he began to train in track to improve his general conditioning, however, he realized that it was a demanding physical discipline. He became a strong competitive runner, winning both the Kansas two-mile and one-mile championships twice in a row.

After Mills graduated from high school, the University of Kansas awarded him a full athletic scholarship. He became a star on the track team that won national championships twice, but when he tried and failed to qualify for the 1960 Olympic team, he left college never expecting to run again competitively.

Mills joined the U.S. Marines, and he began running again. After he won the interservice 10,000-meter race, the marines sent Mills, still an unknown athlete, to the Olympic trials for the 1964 Olympic Games, to be held in Tokyo, Japan. He made the U.S. team.

The odds on Mills winning a gold medal in his race, the 10,000-meter, were about a thousand to one. During the early stage of the race, he was pushed by other runners and dropped behind. Before long, however, he regained his stride, and he took the lead in the home stretch. Then, he was passed by two other runners, and it seemed as if he had no chance of winning. Suddenly, he kicked in with a tremendous sprint, and he regained the lead with about 260 feet (80 m) to go. With the crowd roaring at this stunning development,

Mills won the race, in a time of 28:24.4. He had improved his own previous best time by nearly one minute, and he had also set a new Olympic record.

When Mills returned home from the Olympics, the Lakota honored him with a ring made of gold from the Black Hills. The ring reminded Mills that those who achieve great things have a responsibility to give something back to their community. Since his Olympic triumph, he has done just that. For years, he has visited nearly every reservation and urban Native center in the United States and has traveled to more than fifty other countries to speak about Native American issues.

Mills also serves as national spokesperson for Running Strong, Christian Relief Services' American Indian Youth division, which raises money for food, medicine, and clothing for reservations.

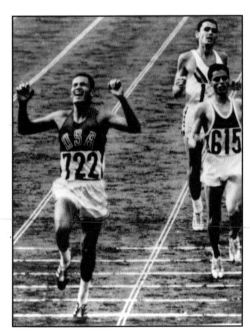

Billy Mills winning the 10,000-meter race at the 1964 Olympic Games

90

Along with fellow activist Janet McCloud (see no. 79), Ramona Bennett played an important part in the struggle to defend the fishing rights of Northwest Native Americans.

Bennett grew up in Seattle and attended public school there, but she felt out of place. She was often depressed. Then, she says, her life turned around after she visited the Seattle Indian Center and began volunteering with the Indian Service League.

In the 1950s, Bennett moved to the Puyallup Reservation. There were few jobs, and the community was very poor. Bennett was determined to change this situation. In the 1960s, she was elected to the Puyallup Tribal Council, and she began lobbying the U.S. Congress about problems on the reservation.

"If I couldn't get an appointment with a Congressman," she has said, "I'd wait outside his door for the bell to ring calling him to vote—and when he came out, I'd run with him." The tribal council could not often afford round-trip tickets to Washington, D.C., so afterward, Bennett would sometimes hitchhike the 3,000 miles (4,800 km) home.

During the 1960s, the Puyallup depended on fishing, because few people on the reservation had jobs. Fishing, however, put them in conflict with state fishing conservation regulations. With Janet McCloud, Bennett helped to found the Survival of American Indians Association to defend Native fishing rights. In 1970, the state banned fishing traps and sent law enforcement agents to stop the Puyallup from fishing. State officials took the traps and jailed the fishermen.

Bennett and others set up an armed camp on the riverbank to defend the fishermen. After ten weeks, agents raided the camp using tear gas and clubs. They arrested Bennett and the

Ramona Bennett

others and charged them with incitement to riot. The protesters faced a possible thirty-five years in prison. The case was thrown out of court when the Secretary of the Interior stated that the agents had been trespassing on Puyallup land. Later, courts ruled that Native Americans had a right to half of the fish caught in Washington coastal waters.

In 1972, Bennett was elected chairperson of the Puyallup Tribal Council. Only a few women headed tribal councils at the time, and the National Tribal Chairman's Association tried to deny her admittance to their meeting, asking her to sit with the chairmen's wives. Bennett had to push her way in. Once she was in, she demanded that the association make the needs of children a high priority.

Bennett left the tribal council after eight years as chairperson and began devoting herself to the needs of minority children. She became the executive director of Rainbow Youth and Family Services, an organization she established to help children of color resist being adopted outside their home communities.

85. Clyde Bellecourt
(1939–)

Clyde Bellecourt

As a cofounder of the American Indian Movement (AIM), Clyde Bellecourt has focused on fighting for Native American rights, teaching young people about Native American history, and educating the American public about conditions on reservations.

Bellecourt grew up in Minnesota, on an Ojibwa reservation. He dropped out of school after the ninth grade and moved to the city to try to find work. When he was unable to find a job, he began committing robberies. Finally, he ended up in Minnesota's Stillwater State Prison. Depressed, Bellecourt started a hunger fast. Another inmate, Eddie Benton Banai, began dropping a candy bar into Bellecourt's cell every day. Bellecourt didn't touch them, and the pile grew.

One day, Banai brought him a book about the Ojibwa instead. It caught Bellecourt's interest. He ended his hunger strike and eventually started teaching other Native American prisoners about Native culture and history.

In 1968, Bellecourt, along with Banai, George Mitchell, and Dennis Banks (see no. 75), founded AIM. At first, AIM's main goal was to protect Native Americans in Minneapolis from police brutality. Bellecourt formed a street patrol that monitored police calls, filmed arrests of Native Americans, and informed those being arrested about their right to an attorney. The patrols greatly reduced the number of Native Americans arrested.

Next, AIM activists put together schools for Native American children. The schools offered students an education in Native American culture and history to counteract what AIM members claimed was the biased presentation in American history textbooks. Native American elders taught students spiritual ceremonies that had previously been outlawed.

AIM then began to engage in what Bellecourt called "confrontational politics." In 1969, about two hundred AIM activists took over the abandoned prison on Alcatraz Island, in San Francisco Bay. They stated that it would be a "suitable" place for a reservation and offered to buy it for cheap jewelry worth twenty-four dollars—the sum for which Manhattan Island had been bought from the Indians.

In 1973, AIM members took over the village of Wounded Knee, causing the federal government to besiege the town. Many AIM activists at Wounded Knee armed themselves, but Bellecourt, a pacifist, refused to carry a weapon.

Like other leaders, Bellecourt was arrested and charged for his activities at Wounded Knee, but the charges were dropped. In the mid-1970s, Bellecourt returned to AIM's earlier project, founding schools. He helped to establish several alternative schools for Native Americans throughout the country.

In 1979, Bellecourt helped found the American Indian Opportunities Industrial Center, the first school in the United States to offer vocational training specifically for Native Americans. In the 1980s and 1990s, he organized several youth service centers.

A writer, Paula Gunn Allen has spent much of her life trying to increase the recognition of the Native American literary tradition.

Allen has described her birth as a "multicultural event." She grew up in a Laguna Pueblo community near Albuquerque, New Mexico, but her ancestors are Pueblo, Sioux, Lebanese, and Scottish-American. She was raised mostly by her mother and grandmother, and she grew up taking for granted the respected place of women in Laguna Pueblo culture.

Allen has said that until she became involved with the feminist movement in the 1960s and 1970s, she did not realize that women were not equally respected in the Western tradition. She remarked, "I grew up with the notion that women are strong. I didn't know that I was supposed to be silly and weak."

As a child, Allen attended mission schools, and for high school, she went to a Catholic boarding school. She started college at the University of New Mexico and then transferred to the University of Oregon, where she began writing poetry. In Oregon, she began to experience what writer N. Scott Momaday (see no. 80) calls "land-sickness." She was so homesick for her Laguna community that she became depressed.

Reading Momaday's book *House Made of Dawn* helped her to understand what was happening to her. After finishing her master's degree, Allen married and had three children. The marriage ended in divorce, and after two more failed marriages, she came to the realization that she was a lesbian.

Returning to the University of New Mexico, Allen thought she would pursue a Ph.D. in Native American literature, but according to her dean, Native American literature did not exist. Allen completed her degree in American studies instead, and she began a career as a college profes-

sor. Over the years, she has taught at the University of New Mexico; the University of California, Berkeley; and the University of California, Los Angeles.

While she was still in school, Allen published a book of poetry. Since then, she has written several more volumes of poetry and a novel. At the same time, Allen has also worked to educate the public about Native American literature.

In 1983, she edited an anthology of essays and course designs on Native American literature. She has also edited two anthologies of Native American literature, one of which, *Spider Woman's Granddaughters*, won the American Book Award in 1990.

Allen may be best known for her 1986 book, *The Sacred Hoop*. A groundbreaking contribution to feminist literature, the book is a study of Native traditions that center on women.

Paula Gunn Allen

William Hensley

One of the founders of the Alaska Federation of Natives, William Hensley was instrumental in helping convince the U.S. Congress to pass the Alaska Native Claims Settlement Act of 1971.

Hensley was born in Kotzebue, Alaska, to an Inupiat family. As a child, he attended elementary school in Alaska, but then he was removed from his family and taken to a boarding school in Knoxville, Tennessee. At the time, the Bureau of Indian Affairs had a policy of removing children from their families, sometimes forcibly, and placing them in boarding schools where teachers tried to make them abandon their culture.

Hensley attended several colleges before transferring to George Washington University, in Washington, D.C., where he graduated in 1966. Returning to Alaska, Hensley took a course on constitutional law and wrote a paper called, "What Rights to Land Have the Alaska Native?"

At the time, leaders of regional Native groups were beginning to organize. Hensley mailed copies of his paper to village leaders in the Kotzebue area. As Hensley's paper was passed around, he found himself closely involved in the land claims dispute. He attended meetings with village leaders from the Kotzebue region, and in 1966, he helped to found the Northwest Alaska Native Association (NANA) to protect the interests of Alaska Natives in that area.

The same year, Hensley helped to found the Alaska Federation of Natives (AFN). He became the executive director, president, and cochairman of the AFN. The organization lobbied Congress to pass the Alaska Native Claims Settlement Act of 1971, recognizing Alaska Native rights to 44 million acres (17 million ha) of land and providing one billion dollars to organize thirteen Native corporations to manage Native money and land. NANA became one of the new Native corporations, and Hensley became its executive director and chairman.

In 1966, Hensley was elected as a representative to the Alaska State Legislature, and in 1970, he became a state senator. During his early years in the legislature, he continued to work on behalf of AFN and the land claims struggle, but he also worked on other issues.

As a state senator, Hensley represented twenty thousand people in a district that was slightly larger than the state of Montana. Few villages in the area had electricity. Hensley founded the Alaska Village Electric Cooperative, which shortly thereafter hooked up electricity to fifty villages that had never had it.

Hensley left office in 1974, but he returned in 1986 and stayed for two years. In 1987, he pushed the Alaska Legislature to form a committee on suicide prevention. The committee investigated the issue of suicide in rural Alaska, which has one of the highest suicide rates in the country, and it formed a long-term suicide prevention program.

Poet Simon Ortiz was one of the writers who laid the groundwork for the Native American literary renaissance of the 1960s and 1970s.

Ortiz spent his early childhood years in a small village near Acoma Pueblo, in New Mexico. At first, he spoke only Acoma, but at his school, teachers hit students on the back or knuckles if they spoke their own language. So, Ortiz learned English. Despite the harsh treatment, Ortiz was excited about attending school, because he loved stories and loved learning to read.

After the sixth grade, Ortiz was sent to St. Catherine's boarding school, in Santa Fe, New Mexico. Teachers there tried to convert students to Catholicism. Ortiz was disappointed, but he escaped into his books. He wrote in a diary and read anything he could find, even the dictionary. He did not consider becoming a writer, because he knew of no Native American writers. Instead, he decided to learn a trade and took classes in sheet metal and woodworking.

After graduating from high school, Ortiz began work as a laborer in the uranium industry. In 1962, he left to go to college, using a Bureau of Indian Affairs grant and his savings. At about this time, he began drinking. "No one could tell me the dangers of alcohol use," he said later, "and I was arrogant enough to think I could control it."

Frustrated by his college experience, Ortiz joined the U.S. Army. He decided to return to school when he got out. He enrolled at the University of New Mexico but quit in 1968. At about this time, Ortiz became aware of Native American political activists, and he was inspired by the book *House Made of Dawn*, by N. Scott Momaday (see no. 80).

In 1969, Ortiz completed a master of fine arts degree at the University of Iowa and was "discovered" by the National Endowment for the Arts, which gave him a journalism award.

He began writing poetry during the 1970s. His first book of poetry, *Going for the Rain*, came out in 1976, the same year as the book *Ceremony*, by Leslie Marmon Silko (see no. 96). Together, the works of Momaday, Silko, and Ortiz marked a new period of Native American literature.

Ortiz writes his poems to be read aloud. He tries not to express his own individual interests in his work. Instead, he writes with the voice of the community. He has also tried to raise public awareness about Native American issues.

By the 1990s, Ortiz had written fourteen books, and the Gift Festival of Native Writers awarded him a Lifetime Achievement Award. His work has influenced several other important writers, including Joy Harjo (see no. 97) and Sherman Alexie (see no. 100).

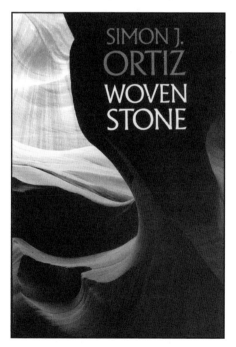

The cover of Simon Ortiz's book
Woven Stone

89. Buffy Sainte-Marie
(1941–)

Buffy Sainte-Marie

Award-winning singer and songwriter Buffy Sainte-Marie has spent much of her career celebrating the joys of Native American life and raising public awareness about the problems Native Americans face.

Sainte-Marie was born to Cree parents in Saskatchewan, Canada, and was adopted by a part-Micmac couple who raised her in Maine and Massachusetts. At the age of four, Sainte-Marie taught herself to play piano. As a child, she wrote songs easily, and as a teenager, she taught herself to play guitar.

After graduating from high school, she entered the University of Massachusetts. There, she played in coffeehouses and became known for love songs and songs about Native American life and social issues. In 1962, she completed her bachelor's degree. Eventually, she went on to earn a Ph.D. as well.

Sainte-Marie moved to New York City and became part of the explosion of folk culture during the 1960s. She continued to sing in cafes and clubs, but she also released her first record, in 1963. The following year, she played her first Carnegie Hall concert. Critics noted her use of Native vocables, meaningless syllables that are repeated in a tune, and her use of an ancient instrument, the mouthbow. One critic praised her for her exceptional range, saying, "She can sing on, off, or around the pitch, as she chooses; her sense of phrasing is superb."

At about this time, Sainte-Marie became known as a Native American rights activist. Her song "Now That the Buffalo's Gone" is often called the first Native American protest song, and "Starwalker" has been called the theme song of the American Indian Movement (AIM). Sainte-Marie's song "Until It's Time" is one of the world's most recorded songs. Janis Joplin, Barbra Streisand, and Elvis Presley are among the hundreds of artists who have recorded it.

During her career, Sainte-Marie has traveled around the world, and she has become internationally famous. In 1983, she received an Academy Award, a Golden Globe, and Canada's Juno Award for the song "Up Where We Belong." She has received a medal from Queen Elizabeth II, a Lifetime Achievement Award from the American Indian College Fund, and France's award for "Best International Artist." Sainte-Marie is also an Officer in the Order of Canada, that nation's highest civilian honor.

In the late 1980s, Sainte-Marie pioneered a second career, as a digital artist, creating paintings on a computer. She is an Adjunct Professor of Fine Arts at First Nations University of Canada. Her Cradleboard Teaching Project teaches Native American core curriculum online.

Sainte-Marie also continues to perform concerts and to release recordings.

90. Frank Dukepoo
(1943–1999)

Frank Dukepoo was the first Hopi to earn a Ph.D., and at the time, he became one of only a few Native Americans across the country to have a doctorate in the sciences.

Dukepoo grew up at First Mesa on the Mohave Reservation, in Arizona. He grew interested in genetics while listening to the advice of his father, a farmer, about where to plant seeds.

In 1961, Dukepoo entered Arizona State University with several scholarships, but he lost them all when he let his grades fall too low. Racism was a problem on campus, and Dukepoo remembered being called a "dirty, dumb, stupid, drunk Indian." He later said, however, that his biggest problem was that, like many college freshmen, "I had free time and money and didn't know what to do with it." One of Dukepoo's professors pushed him to pull his grades up, and he did. After earning his bachelor's degree, he continued his education, and in 1973, he graduated with a Ph.D. in genetics.

Dukepoo held a variety of zoology and genetics-related jobs. Finally, he joined the faculty of Northern Arizona University. In addition to teaching biology, he directed a National Science Foundation program to encourage Native Americans at the university to stay in school. While he was the director, not a single student in the program dropped out.

Still, Dukepoo wanted to do more, and in 1982, he founded the National Native American Honor Society. To join this organization, Native American students must earn straight As for at least one semester. By 1991, hundreds of students in the Southwest were members of NNAHS. Dukepoo also helped to found two organizations devoted to encouraging minority students, the Society for the Advancement of Chicanos and Native Americans in Science and the American Indian Science and Engineering Society.

At the same time, Dukepoo was conducting his own research. He researched birth defects among Southwestern Native Americans, and his study of albinism among the Hopi became a classic in the field. When the Human Genome Project began, Dukepoo was on the verge of mapping the gene for albinism among the Hopi.

Dukepoo was concerned, however, about what the Genome Project would mean to Native Americans. He knew that, historically, the scientific community has not always behaved ethically toward Native peoples. Archaeologists have stolen bones from Native Americans, for example, and in the past, doctors have sterilized Native American women without their consent.

So Dukepoo put his own research on hold. He began working with the Human Genome Project to make sure that indigenous peoples were treated ethically by researchers. His work was cut short when he died suddenly, of natural causes, in 1999.

Frank Dukepoo

Leonard Peltier

Leonard Peltier may be the most well-known federal prisoner in the United States. Since his controversial 1975 conviction for murdering two FBI agents, millions of people around the world have petitioned for his release.

Peltier is Ojibwa and French. He was born into a family of migrant workers. When he was four years old, his parents separated, and he went to live with his grandparents. With them, he moved back and forth between logging camps and copper mines.

When Peltier was about nine, a man drove up suddenly while he was outside playing. He recalls, "My grandmother started crying and told us this man was here to take us to Wahpeton Indian School." Peltier and his sister and cousin left for Wahpeton, where school officials cut their hair, stripped them, and poured powdered DDT on them. Peltier stayed at the boarding school until his mother could afford to care for him. Shortly afterward,

he went to live with his father at the Turtle Mountain Reservation.

In 1959, Peltier moved to the Pacific Northwest. By the time he was twenty, he co-owned and operated an auto body shop in Seattle. He joined activists such as Ramona Bennett (see no. 84) to work on behalf of Northwest Native fishing rights. In the 1970s, he joined the American Indian Movement (AIM).

In 1972, Peltier got into a fight with an off-duty police officer in Milwaukee and was charged with attempted murder. He jumped bail and went underground. On South Dakota's Pine Ridge Reservation, meanwhile, some elders accused the tribal president of corruption and of arming his own private police force. Violent incidents began to occur frequently, and the elders asked AIM for help. Along with Dennis Banks (see no. 75), Clyde Bellecourt (see no. 85), and other activists, Peltier occupied the site of Wounded Knee on the reservation, to protest injustices against Native Americans. Later, Peltier and others established a camp at the town of Oglala to protect people.

In 1975, two FBI agents drove toward the camp at Oglala, following Peltier and two other AIM activists, who were in a truck. There was a shoot-out, and someone shot both agents at close range, killing them. Peltier was tried and convicted of the murders and sentenced to two consecutive life-terms in prison.

After the trial, there was an outpouring of support for Peltier. Dennis Banks, AIM, Amnesty International, and other groups have called for his release. Some people believe he is innocent, and others believe that he should be freed because there were irregularities in his trial. Peltier lost what may have been his best chance for freedom when outgoing U.S. president Bill Clinton refused to grant him a pardon in 2001.

92. Michael Dorris
(1945–1997)

Writer Michael Dorris, who was part Modoc Indian, won several awards for his books. After a longtime struggle with depression, his career was tragically cut short by suicide.

When Dorris was two years old, his father died. His mother never remarried, and she raised Dorris with help from his two grandmothers and three aunts. They lived in Kentucky, but Dorris also visited his father's family frequently, in Tacoma, Washington, and on reservations in the Pacific Northwest.

Growing up, Dorris attended Catholic schools. He chose Georgetown University, a Catholic school, for college as well. He graduated with honors in English and then pursued a degree in anthropology from Yale. In 1971, he traveled to Tyonek, Alaska, to do field research for his master's degree, studying the impact of oil revenues on a fishing village.

Dorris was lonely in Alaska and decided to apply to adopt a child. He adopted a three-year-old Lakota Sioux boy, whom he named Abel. The boy had a host of physical and behavioral problems that were later diagnosed as fetal alcohol syndrome. In 1972, the two moved to Dartmouth University, where Dorris founded the school's Native American Studies Program. While living there, he adopted two more children.

In May 1979, Dorris and his children met Louise Erdrich (see no. 98). Dorris had a grant to study the Maori in New Zealand, however, and he and the children went there for seven months. Finally, in 1981, Dorris and Erdrich were married. She adopted Dorris's children, and the couple had three more children of their own.

Dorris and Erdrich were both writers, and they began showing each other drafts of their manuscripts and commenting extensively on them. They developed a strong collaborative relationship, although they continued to publish books under their individual names only.

They both wrote extensively during their marriage, receiving many awards for their works.

Dorris continued teaching at Dartmouth, but he was also Erdrich's agent for her book *Love Medicine*. In 1989, he wrote a study of fetal alcohol syndrome, *The Broken Cord*, based on Abel's experiences. The book won a National Book Critic Circle Award. Two years later, tragedy struck the family when Abel was hit by a car and killed.

In the 1990s, Dorris won acclaim for his children's books. *Morning Girl*, a young adult novel, won the Scott O'Dell Award for Historical Fiction, and *Guests* was an ALA Notable Book of the Year.

Dorris's personal life, however, began to unravel. Several of his children accused him of abuse. Erdrich moved out, later commenting that Dorris had struggled with depression for years and that she could not support him any longer. In 1997, Dorris committed suicide.

Michael Dorris

93. John Echohawk
(1945–)

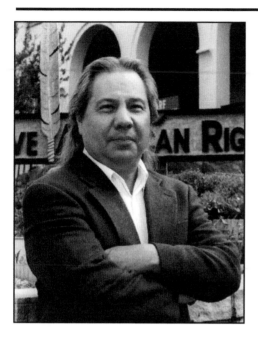

John Echohawk

John Echohawk is a founder and executive director of the Native American Rights Fund (NARF), an organization that provides legal help to Native Americans and to Native American nations and organizations.

He was born in Albuquerque, New Mexico, to a distinguished Pawnee family. His grandfather was a scout for the U.S. Cavalry in the late 1800s. His uncle, painter and actor Brummett Echohawk, painted the famous picture *Trail of Tears*, which depicts the Cherokee as they were forced to relocate to Oklahoma during the 1830s.

Echohawk grew up attending public school in New Mexico. He was one of six children, three of whom became lawyers. He came of age during the 1960s, and Martin Luther King Jr. became one of his heroes. After receiving a special scholarship to attend college from a new federal program for training Native lawyers, Echohawk became the program's first graduate.

In law school, he cofounded the American Indian Law Students Association.

In 1970, Echohawk graduated from law school. That year, the Ford Foundation provided a grant to the California Indian Legal Services (CILS) to establish a legal defense fund for Native Americans. CILS hired Echohawk to work on the project, and the Native American Rights Fund was born.

Echohawk transformed NARF into a powerful organization. As its executive director, he has supervised as many as fifty cases at a time, while also raising seven million dollars a year to pay for NARF's services. The organization has won hundreds of cases since its inception.

In 1989, for example, Echohawk won a case for the Catawba, enabling them to recover 144,000 acres (58,275 ha) of North Carolina land. In 1992, he won a federal district court case, affirming the jurisdiction of tribal courts to hear civil matters on tribal lands in North Dakota. The same year, he forced Montana to recognize the Northern Cheyenne's right to 90,000 acre-feet of water.

In 1996, NARF filed the largest class action suit ever against the federal government, demanding that the Bureau of Indian Affairs explain what has happened to billions of dollars that it has held and managed for Native Americans during the last one hundred years. The account is a trust fund comprised of money paid by non-Natives to use Native land. According to the suit, the BIA did not know how much money had been collected and failed to "provide even a basic, regular statement to Indian account holders." Several years later, the case was still in the courts.

Echohawk has received many awards for his leadership in the field of law. The National Law Journal has named him as one of the "100 Most Influential Lawyers in America," and the American Bar Association has given him its "Spirit of Excellence" award.

Wilma Mankiller was the first woman to be elected as principal chief of the Cherokee nation. She was the sixth of eleven children in her family. The family lived on Cherokee land in Tahlequah, Oklahoma, in a four-room house that had no electricity and no running water. When she was ten years old, her family relocated to San Francisco. The experience was a tremendous culture shock for everyone.

In San Francisco, Mankiller graduated from high school, got married, and had two children. She also began working with Indian civil rights activists. In 1969, members of the American Indian Movement (AIM) and other activists occupied Alcatraz. Mankiller began to show her skill as an organizer by raising money and supplies for people participating in the occupation.

After the Alcatraz occupation ended, Mankiller threw herself into volunteer work with new energy. In 1974, she and her husband divorced, and she and her two daughters returned to Tahlequah. There, Mankiller began working for the Cherokee nation and attending college. One morning, she was in a car accident that shattered her face, legs, and ribs. The other car's driver, who was killed in the crash, was Mankiller's best friend.

After she recovered from the accident, as well as from a severe illness that required surgery and steroid therapy, Mankiller finally returned to her job with the Cherokee nation, in 1980. One of her first projects was to organize volunteers and raise funds to build a water line for the town of Bell, which did not have running water and was one of the poorest Cherokee communities.

In 1983, Cherokee chief Ross Swimmer asked Mankiller to run with him in his bid for reelection, as his deputy chief. Mankiller feared that people would think she was too liberal. The hate mail and death threats she received, however, were due to her gender. Mankiller later noted that the Cherokee had learned sexism from Europeans. Traditionally, Cherokee women were always involved in government.

Swimmer and Mankiller won the election despite the controversy over her candidacy. In 1985, Swimmer resigned, and Mankiller became the first woman ever to be principal chief of the Cherokee nation. She narrowly won reelection in 1987, but she got 82 percent of the vote in 1992.

As chief, Mankiller's had to make sure that Cherokee laws were enforced, work with the tribal council to pass legislation, and supervise Cherokee-run programs. She spent much of her time writing grants for health and education programs, including the Cherokee Home Health Agency and Head Start.

Throughout her tenure as chief, Mankiller struggled with kidney disease. Then, in 1995, Mankiller was diagnosed with lymphoma, and she did not run for reelection. In 1998, U.S. president Bill Clinton awarded her the Presidential Medal of Freedom.

Wilma Mankiller

Robert Eugene Megginson

Robert Eugene Megginson is one of only a few Native Americans in the United States to have completed a doctoral degree in mathematics. He has devoted much of his life to encouraging Native American students to study math.

Megginson grew up in a family that appreciated mathematics. His father, whose family was English, had a bachelor's degree in physics and math. His Lakota grandfather was very knowledgeable about mathematics and often gave him math problems to work out for fun.

At school, teachers and students were sometimes surprised when Megginson's abilities did not match their preconception of what a Native American should be like. Some teachers also had low expectations of Megginson because his family was not well off financially.

Although tests eventually showed that Megginson was about four grade levels ahead of his class, he was once placed in a "slow" section of a class because the teacher assumed that a child with his background could not be a good student. Later, Megginson reflected that teachers all too often do lower their expectations in this way, sending a message, intentionally or not, that "because you are both American Indian and economically disadvantaged, you are doomed to do poorly in school." Fortunately, Megginson also encountered other teachers who recognized his abilities and encouraged him.

In college, at the University of Illinois at Urbana-Champaign, Megginson did not immediately turn to mathematics. Initially, he completed a degree in physics and began working as a computer software specialist. In 1977, however, he decided to return to school, pursuing a master's degree in statistics and a Ph.D. in mathematics. He became a teacher, first joining the faculty of Eastern Illinois University and later moving to the University of Michigan at Ann Arbor.

As a mathematician, Megginson has studied multidimensional spaces. In addition, he has worked to make it possible for other Native American students to follow in his footsteps. He is a member of several organizations that encourage minority participation in mathematics and often plan programs aimed at Native American students. In 1992, he developed a summer program for high school students at the Turtle Mountain Indian Reservation in North Dakota. The program stresses the connections between mathematics and traditional Ojibwa culture.

In 1997, Megginson received the U.S. Presidential Award for Excellence in Science, Mathematics, and Engineering Mentoring. In 1999, the American Indian Science and Engineering Society awarded him its Ely S. Parker Lifetime Achievement Award. He was named to the Native American Science and Engineering Wall of Fame in 2001.

Leslie Marmon Silko has been called "the most accomplished Indian writer of her generation." Silko was born in Albuquerque, New Mexico, and she was raised on the Old Laguna Pueblo Reservation. She is of Laguna Pueblo, European, Plains Native, and Mexican ancestry. Among the Laguna, women play important roles. Laguna women traditionally own property, and Laguna gods are female. Not surprisingly, Silko was surrounded by strong female role models.

Silko's grandmother was a mechanic who fixed machines in her son's laundry even as an elderly woman. Silko's father encouraged Silko and her sisters to take part in traditionally male activities, such as hunting. As a child, Silko helped round up the family's cattle, and she had her own horse by the time she was eight years old.

Silko attended the local Bureau of Indian Affairs school as a child but commuted to a Catholic school in Albuquerque as a teenager. Then, she attended the University of New Mexico. While there, she married and had a son. Busy as a parent, she decided to take a creative writing class she thought would be easy. It was the beginning of her career as a writer.

In 1971, she was awarded a grant from the National Endowment for the Arts based on a story she had originally written for class. By the time she received her NEA grant, she was in law school, but the grant convinced her to drop out and focus on her writing.

Silko began teaching at Navajo Community College in Tsaile, Arizona, and she published a book of poems. Then, she moved to Ketchikan, Alaska, where she wrote *Ceremony*, a book that is often compared to *House Made of Dawn*,

the Pulitzer Prize-winning novel by N. Scott Momaday (see no. 80). Both books concern a Native American veteran adjusting to life at home after World War II. *Ceremony* ends on a more optimistic note than Momaday's novel, however, presenting Native traditions as a way to heal and regain one's sanity.

After leaving Alaska, Silko returned to the Southwest, becoming a professor first at the University of New Mexico and then at the University of Arizona. During this time, she became friends with the poet James Wright. After Wright died of cancer, his widow published Silko's and Wright's letters to each other, and the book won the prize for nonfiction from the *Boston Globe* newspaper.

In 1981, Silko was awarded the MacArthur Foundation's fellowship, which is often called a "genius grant." She used the money to support herself as she wrote her most controversial novel, *Almanac of the Dead*, which focuses on the history of genocide in the Americas. Since the publication of this book, she has written another novel and a book of essays.

The cover of Leslie Marmon Silko's book *Storyteller*

Joy Harjo

Joy Harjo is one of the foremost poets of the Native American literary renaissance that began in the 1960s. In addition to being a poet, she is a screenwriter, jazz musician, and teacher.

Harjo was born in Tulsa, Oklahoma, where her Creek ancestors had relocated when the federal government forced the Creek to give up their lands in Alabama and Georgia in the nineteenth century. An imaginative child, she pretended that the oil wells in her neighborhood were monsters.

During her youth, Harjo hoped to become a missionary, and she practiced preaching to the children of her neighborhood. She gave up her plans, however, after she watched her local minister ask two Mexican girls to leave church because they were too noisy. She left with them and didn't go back.

When Harjo was sixteen, she began attending a boarding school, the Institute of American Indian Arts (IAIA), in Santa Fe, New Mexico. There, she took up painting, and after hearing readings by Leslie Marmon Silko (see no. 96) and Simon Ortiz (see no. 88), she was also inspired to begin writing poetry. Then, she went on to college, at the University of New Mexico at Albuquerque, where she studied painting and creative writing.

Harjo also bore her two children while studying there, the first in 1968 and the second in 1973. To support herself and her children, she worked as a waitress, gas-station attendant, and nurse's assistant. After graduating, Harjo earned her master's in fine arts from the University of Iowa, and she began teaching at universities, including the University of Arizona and the University of New Mexico.

During her years of teaching, Harjo was also writing poetry. She published several books of poetry, and her 1983 volume, *She Had Some Horses*, remained in print for more than a decade and is often used in college literature courses. She has often written about the history of exploitation and oppression in the Americas, including both the Native American genocide and the Reconstruction-era lynchings of African Americans after the Civil War.

When Harjo was in her thirties, she began teaching herself to play the saxophone with the help of Jim Pepper, a Creek/Kaw jazz saxophonist. She began playing soprano and alto saxophone with an all Native American band called Poetic Justice. The band's music accompanies Harjo's readings of her poetry on a CD that comes with the 1994 edition of her book, *The Woman Who Fell from the Sky*.

Harjo has received many awards for her poetry, including the William Carlos Williams Award of the Poetry Society of America and the Lifetime Achievement Award from the Native Writers Circle of the Americas.

Louise Erdrich is one of the most noted Native American writers of the twentieth century. Part Ojibwa, she is best known for the books she has written portraying life among the Ojibwa, such as *Love Medicine, The Beet Queen,* and *The Bingo Palace.*

Erdrich grew up in Wahpeton, a town near the North Dakota and Minnesota border. Her parents taught in Bureau of Indian Affairs schools, and they encouraged Erdrich to write. Her father paid her a nickel for each story, and her mother bound the stories into little books with construction-paper covers.

Erdrich was raised Catholic and attended Catholic public schools, but she learned about Ojibwa traditions from her grandfather. Although he was also Catholic, Erdrich has said that he went into the woods to pray, not church, and that he prayed in Ojibwa. Once, she said, her grandfather told her that he was praying for a safe landing on the Moon. She admired his ability to combine traditional practices with modern life.

Erdrich attended Dartmouth College, where Michael Dorris (see no. 92) was teaching, but she did not begin her relationship with him until much later. After completing her B.A., Erdrich took any job she could find that would allow her time to write. She sold popcorn at movie theaters, worked as a lifeguard, and waited tables.

In 1977, Erdrich completed a master's degree in fine arts at Johns Hopkins University. She wrote fiction and edited the newspaper of the Boston Indian Council. She met Dorris in 1980, and the couple married in 1981. Erdrich then adopted the three children that Dorris had already adopted.

Erdrich's relationship with Dorris helped both of them become more productive in their literary careers. They collaborated on most of their works, with one writing a first draft of a piece and the other reading it over and commenting on it. Dorris also acted as an agent for Erdrich's first book, *Love Medicine,* which won the National Book Critics Circle Award in 1984.

For many years, Erdrich and Dorris were famous for their seemingly perfect collaborative relationship. Besides writing together, the couple devoted themselves to their family. They raised three children of their own, in addition to their three adopted children.

Louise Erdrich

During the 1990s, however, their relationship began to fall apart. Erdrich later said that Dorris had been depressed and suicidal for years. In 1997, Erdrich decided to leave him, and he faced allegations of child abuse. The abuse charge was never investigated because Dorris committed suicide.

After Dorris's death, Erdrich began to put her life back together. She kept writing, and she produced a new novel, *The Last Report on the Miracles at Little No Horse.*

An activist and writer, Winona LaDuke has twice run as the Green party candidate for the office of vice president of the United States.

LaDuke grew up on the West Coast. Her mother, a Jewish art professor, and her father, an Ojibwa actor, were both antiwar activists during the Vietnam War, and she became interested in politics at an early age.

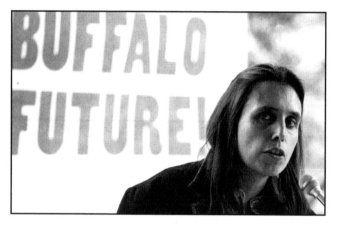

Winona LaDuke

As a teenager, LaDuke began studying the impact of mining and multinational corporations on reservations. When she was eighteen, she presented her research before the United Nations. Afterward, she alternated between her studies at Harvard University and work on reservations. Eventually, LaDuke graduated from Harvard with degrees in Native economic development and rural development.

After graduating, she moved to the area from which her family came, the White Earth Reservation, in northern Minnesota. She became the principal for the Circle of Life School on the reservation, and she began working on a lawsuit to recover Ojibwa lands from logging companies and the federal government. When the lawsuit failed, LaDuke founded the White Earth Land Recovery Project, an organization that buys back Ojibwa land an

acre at a time. To begin the project, she used the money from the International Reebok Human Rights Award, which she won in 1989.

In 1994, *Time* magazine named LaDuke one of the fifty most promising leaders in the United States under the age of forty. In 1996, the Green party asked her to run for president of the United States. She refused, but she did agree to run for vice president as consumer advocate Ralph Nader's running mate. The two headed the Green party ticket once again in the 2000 presidential election.

In 2000, LaDuke campaigned while nursing a baby, her third child. She and Nader had won only one percent of the vote in 1996, but in 2000, they drew almost three percent of the national vote. In some states, such as Oregon and California, the percentage was even higher.

The votes they received may have changed the outcome of the 2000 election. Many analysts believe that Nader and LaDuke attracted left-leaning voters who would otherwise have voted for Democrat Al Gore, and the result was that Republican George W. Bush won the election. More importantly for their supporters, Nader and LaDuke catapulted the Green Party into national prominence, making it a viable third-party option in many states.

In between elections, LaDuke has devoted much of her time to research, writing, and activism. She has written many articles on Native American issues and the environment, as well as the novel *Last Standing Woman* (1997) and a nonfiction book about the environment, *All Our Relations* (1999). In 1997, *Ms.* magazine named LaDuke "Woman of the Year."

Sherman Alexie is one of the most prolific and original writers of the Native American literary renaissance.

Mostly of Coeur d'Alene and Spokane descent, Alexie grew up on the Spokane Indian Reservation, in a family of alcoholics. He worked hard to avoid alcohol as a teenager. Alexie loved books so much that his parents transferred him to a mostly white high school in a nearby town, where he could take college preparatory courses that were not available on the reservation.

At the age of eighteen, Alexie began attending Gonzaga University. He stayed for two years and then transferred to Washington State University. In college, he began drinking heavily. "I guess I was just a lot more confident as a 16-year-old than I was as a 19-year-old," he said later. "I was scared. Alcohol numbs fears."

Alexie did make time to write poetry and short stories, however, and his WSU writing teacher, Alex Kuo, encouraged him to start submitting his work for publication. He was quickly published in the *Beloit Poetry Journal*, *Esquire* magazine, *New York Quarterly*, and several other publications.

After college, Alexie published five books in just over two years. The first book, published in 1991, was *I Would Steal Horses*, a book of poetry. The day it was accepted for publication, he quit drinking. The following year, the book won a prestigious poetry award, and Alexie was awarded a National Endowment for the Arts poetry grant.

The same year, he published another book of poetry, *The Business of Fancydancing*. It was named a Notable Book of the Year by the *New York Times*, which called Alexie "one of the major lyric voices of our time." Critics praised Alexie's use of humor and his use of repetition in his poetry.

Early in 1993, Alexie published two more books of poetry, *Old Shirts & New Skins* and *First Indian on the Moon*, and a book of short stories, *The Lone Ranger and Tonto Fistfight in Heaven*. The book of short stories won two awards for best first book of fiction.

In recent years, Alexie has turned to other forms of writing. He has written the novels *Reservation Blues* and *Indian Killer*. Alexie has also worked in film. *Smoke Signals*, a movie Alexie wrote and produced, won the Audience Award and Filmmakers Trophy at the 1998 Sundance Film Festival.

Alexie is often criticized for portraying Native American alcoholism and hopelessness. Yet Alexie, who is an ardent pacifist, often ends his stories with a note of optimism, such as the following: "… she held the child born of white mother and red father and said, 'Both sides of this baby are beautiful.'"

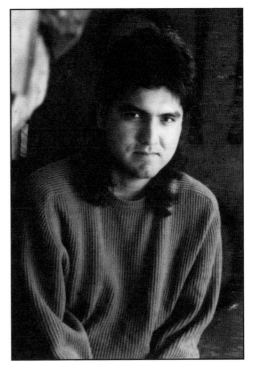

Sherman Alexie

TRIVIA QUIZ

Test your knowledge and challenge your friends with the following questions. The answers are contained in the biographies noted.

1. Which early-seventeenth-century Native American helped bring peace between her people and the first English settlers in America? (see no. 4)

2. Which eighteenth-century Iroquois founded a new religion that is still practiced by many of his people today? (see no. 9)

3. How did a Native American create a system of writing for the Cherokee language that became universally adopted by the entire Cherokee nation? (see no. 13)

4. Who was the Native American woman who served as a guide to the explorers Lewis and Clark on their journey to explore the Louisiana Purchase? (see no. 17)

5. Where did the famous Seminole leader Osceola lead his people's resistance against the U.S. government's efforts to relocate them? (see no. 20)

6. Who was the first, and last, Indian leader in the West to win a war against the U.S. government? (see no. 29)

7. When did the most famous battle in history between Native Americans and the U.S. military take place? (see no. 36)

8. How did a famous Nez Percé chief lead his people on the most brilliant retreat in the history of Native American and U.S. military warfare? (see no. 40)

9. When was the first Native American elected to the United States Senate? (see no. 50)

10. Which Native American pitcher is a member of the Baseball Hall of Fame? (see no. 57)

11. Who was the first Native American to receive the Presidential Medal of Freedom? (see no. 63)

12. Why was a World War II hero ultimately remembered as "a hero to everyone but himself?" (see no. 69)

13. Which Native American was the first U.S. ballerina to become internationally famous? (see no. 72)

14. Which writer became the first Native American to win the Pulitzer Prize for fiction? (see no. 80)

15. Who became the first American athlete to win a long distance track event at the Olympic Games? (see no. 83)

16. Why did activists of the American Indian Movement occupy the site of Wounded Knee on the Pine Ridge Reservation in the 1970s? (see no. 91)

SUGGESTED PROJECTS

1. Choose one Native American nation described in several of the biographies. Read as many entries as necessary in order to write a two- or three-paragraph essay about the nation. Describe where the nation made its home and who were its most famous leaders. Provide details about the relations the nation had with the U.S. government over a prolonged period of time. Were there many conflicts or wars? How were they resolved? Were relations peaceful? Was the nation eventually relocated, and did its members accept relocation peacefully or fight against it? In your essay, also describe what happened to one or two of the nation's most notable leaders.

2. Choose one of the people from this book and write a one-page fictional diary entry for one day in that person's life. Pick a day that had some significance for the individual, such as the day he or she received a significant award or achieved some other noteworthy success. Or, choose a day on which the individual met with a personal setback or was frustrated in some way by a lack of success. Describe the person's thoughts and feelings with as much detail as you can.

INDEX

INDEX

INDEX